# And The Flames Did Not Consume Us

## A Rabbi's Journey Through Communal Crisis

**Gary Mazo**

**Rising Star Press**
**Los Altos, California**

Rising Star Press
P.O. Box BB, Los Altos, California 94023
www.RisingStarPress.com



ISBN #0-933670-06-0

Interior design and composition by Joanne Shwed, Backspace Ink.

Cover design by LeVan Fisher Design.

Original illustration "And the flames did not consume us" by Lisa Mazo Greenberg.

This book is dedicated to the memory of Carol Neulander

*THE MEMORY OF THE RIGHTEOUS IS FOR A BLESSING*

*And the flames did not consume us*

LISA MAZO GREENBERG

# Contents

# Acknowledgements

This book was not easy to write. In many ways it was a catharsis after living through five very difficult years. The encouragement and support of my family and friends helped turn this catharsis into my first literary effort.

First and foremost, I thank my wife and best friend, Debbi, who gave me such strength during this crisis. Without her, I don't know how I could have kept myself together. I also thank my kids, Ari, Daniel and Sara. Their understanding during the times I was unavailable to them showed great sensitivity and compassion from ones so young.

I also thank my agent, Glenn Mollette, for believing in me and helping in this venture.

Without Carl Goldman and Rising Star Press, this book might never have been published. Carl allowed me great creative control to tell my story without including all the salacious details that would surely have put the book on the best-seller list. His integrity allowed me to preserve my own.

I thank Congregation M'kor Shalom for many wonderful years as their spiritual leader. While some in the congregation have recently voiced concern over this publication, I trust that after reading it they will see that the integrity and unique identity of their congregation shine through the words on the pages.

Finally, I thank the Cape Cod Synagogue for allowing me to take the time to write and present this book, thereby achieving some closure on this chapter of my life.

# Foreword

Without warning, a storm broke over Cherry Hill, New Jersey in 1994. Fred Neulander, founder, senior rabbi and esteemed teacher at Congregation M'kor Shalom was linked to allegations of adultery and the murder of his wife. The community sank into deep loss, confusion and anger.

Gary Mazo found himself at the center of this crisis. Fred Neulander had been Mazo's mentor and role model, the man he most wanted to work for after his ordination. Being hired as Neulander's assistant meant the attainment of his dream job. But suddenly the young rabbi was thrust with his family into the most difficult situation of his life. His personal and professional pilgrimage as he sought healing for his shattered community is a story of great struggle and profound faith.

The intensity of emotions engendered by these events created a roller coaster of horrific images, feelings of betrayal and sensational stories in the press. The thrust of Rabbi Mazo's narrative is to provide a *functional human boundary* for dealing with these emotions and stories. The message is that in our faith we can find the strength of stable ground amid the tremors; we can find direction and light with which to guide our lives.

This narrative is an important contribution because tragedy, betrayal and human suffering exist, no matter how much we wish they didn't. They are part of living; and dealing with them must be woven into the fabric of life, neither denied nor suppressed. As Rabbi Mazo has stated, grieving is only "truly complete by learning and understanding."

*Stephen R. Treat, DMin*
*Director and CEO*
*Penn Council for Relationships*
*Philadelphia, Pennsylvania*

# Prologue

On Tuesday, November 1, 1994, my life and the life of my congregation changed forever. That night Carol Neulander, the wife of our senior rabbi, was found brutally murdered in her home. Her family, our congregation and our entire community went into shock. The communal grief was unlike anything I had ever experienced in my short career in the rabbinate.

The next day, a thousand mourners came to the synagogue for a memorial service. The following day, two thousand attended the funeral. We were existing in a surreal world, not truly believing what we were going through.

As the traditional seven-day period of mourning known as shiva got underway, grief mingled with fear and anger. Almost immediately, charges of personal misconduct and sexual impropriety formed a cloud over the grieving widower, our rabbi. Allegations of his involvement in the murder itself soon rocked the very core of our souls. I found myself in the middle of what seemed a terrible made-for-TV movie; but this was real.

Within months, while no formal charges were filed in connection with the murder, the rabbi resigned in disgrace amidst continued allegations of misconduct. As the associate rabbi at Congregation M'kor Shalom, I suddenly found myself responsible for the spiritual well-being of a thousand bewildered families. Under normal circumstances, I would probably not have assumed the role of primary spiritual leader to a congregation of that size for another 20 years. I was facing what would certainly be the greatest challenge of my career. Before it was over, we would all struggle with our faith, with God and with Judaism.

The Bible tells us that when Moses was fleeing the house of Pharaoh he happened upon a certain bush in the desert. As he looked closer, Moses saw the bush was burning—yet the flames did not consume it. Moses stopped, looked into the flames and was able to find there the presence of God.

That was our task: to keep hold of our faith amidst the flames which could have very well consumed us.

This book chronicles the spiritual challenge, emotional upheaval and personal journey the congregation and I experienced through this turbulent time. I have included some of the sermons I gave during key moments in the crisis.

My purpose in writing this book was not to exploit a story of tragedy and betrayal—to do so would be deeply unethical, and would only add to the pain of people I once served and continue to love. My goal is twofold: to offer tribute to the power of the human spirit, which was displayed by so many throughout this ordeal; and to demonstrate the power of Judaism to provide light and guidance in the aftermath of tragedy. It is my hope that other faith communities will find strength and renewal from our journey through the valley of darkness.

CHAPTER 1

# The Rabbi and His Wife

I met Rabbi Fred Neulander and his wife Carol in 1983. Debbi, my wife-to-be, and I were students at Brandeis University. Debbi had grown up in Cherry Hill, New Jersey, a suburb of Philadelphia. She took a semester off from school and went back home. She searched for a spiritual home there, and happened upon Congregation M'kor Shalom, which means "Source of Peace." While attending services there, she became friends with the cantor and the rabbi.

It was on a visit to Debbi's family home that I met him for the first time. The rabbi was about 5'4" but seemed much larger. He was an imposing man, powerfully strong, like a weightlifter. His physical presence and the aura that surrounded him were intimidating.

The rabbi had formed this new, cutting-edge synagogue eight years before. He had taken some of his followers and broken off from the other large Reform synagogue in town to form a more traditional, spiritual and informal synagogue. He was a man with great magnetism, and it was easy to see why people followed him.

He was an eloquent speaker with a gift for language, known for including arcane words—words that weren't in the vocabularies of even the most learned in the community—in his sermons.

He could speak. He was passionate when he spoke. At times he seemed almost angry as the words came out of his mouth. He delivered them with such strength and passion that often a white froth formed around his lips.

And he could teach. He had a great love for Jewish texts and his audience clung to each and every revelation. He was a breath of fresh air in contrast to the more humdrum and formal worship experiences in the community.

Soon his "baby," his congregation, grew. There was an excitement, a vitality that seemed to spread from him to those in the congregation. The aura grew larger. But to some he was intimidating and unapproachable. His intellectual abilities coupled with his obvious physical strength were too much for them. People were drawn to him, yet shied away.

There was arrogance there as well. He knew he was a successful rabbi and that his congregation was special. If he was unhappy with someone he did not hold back. Those who witnessed his temper or heard anecdotes about it grew more intimidated.

He had a right to some of that arrogance. He had done what many in the clergy only dream of: formed his own community and surrounded himself with his supporters.

Women found him attractive. He was handsome, strong, intelligent, powerful in demeanor. He seemed to like the attention. Who wouldn't? People talked about his lunchtime meetings with beautiful women, but he seemed to have a well-grounded sense of self and looked past petty conversation. After all, as far as anyone knew, he was deeply in love with his wife.

Carol was a striking woman. She had a strong personality herself and was quick to put him in his place if he said anything out of line. Their bickering had the appearance of a healthy and loving relationship.

Carol had a wonderful sense of humor. She loved to tell "out of school" tales of being a rabbi's wife. Her stories and humor were as captivating as the best of the rabbi's sermons.

She was also independent. She started a baking company out of her home; her talent in the kitchen, especially with baked goods, was critically acclaimed within the community. Soon she and a partner turned that business into a larger enterprise with its own facility. It became *the bakery* in the community, and was quite successful. From what I could tell, the rabbi was supportive and proud of his wife's achievements. I remember that framed in the bathroom of their house was an article from a local magazine raving about Carol's baked goods.

Carol became an important role model for Debbi. As I was contemplating a life as a rabbi, Debbi would face the challenge of a dual role: as a rabbi in her own right; and as the wife of a rabbi. Carol became the person from whom Debbi could learn the realities of congregational life. Carol was honest, at times brutally honest, about the difficulties associated with being married to a rabbi. As the congregation grew, she clearly became resentful of the time it took away from their family life. She was supportive of the rabbi, but did not wish to give more time than necessary to the congregation. She was not the typical rabbi's wife, and we valued her guidance.

At times Carol seemed angry; yet when speaking with people she cared about, she was warm and giving. One thing was very clear: she loved her children dearly, and protected them intensely.

These were three terrific, great-looking kids. The boys bore their mother's striking features and their father's physical strength. The daughter, their oldest, was a confident and beautiful young lady. Carol marveled in the accomplishments of her children. The family was clearly the focus and top priority of her life. Then came the business; then the synagogue. Some in the synagogue were vocal in criticizing her lack of involvement, but she was not about to change her priorities. Debbi and I grew quite close to the entire family. In June of 1985, the rabbi and Carol joined us at our wedding.

We planned to begin our rabbinic training in Israel right after we were married. During that summer, the rabbi, his wife and kids came to Israel for a visit. They spent the Sabbath with us at our meager apartment, and reminisced about the early days of their marriage. They were the model rabbinic family: happy, affectionate, doing a great job of child rearing, and we hoped to emulate them. During that visit, the rabbi and I joked about the synagogue growing so large that he might need an assistant rabbi by the time of my ordination.

In fact, that growth took place far quicker than I imagined. During my second of five years of study, the rabbi hired an assistant. There went my fantasy of working side by side with the man who had become a mentor to me.

We always stopped by the synagogue on our visits back to New Jersey. Time permitting, we would sit and study with the rabbi. We were now conversant in the Hebrew texts and able to truly study *with* him, not just listen and learn *from* him. I think he valued that give and take as much as we did.

By this time, in 1987, his hair had gone gray and he had shaved his beard. He still had the same build and continued his weightlifting and his racquetball games. Word was that he was an animal on the racquetball court and nearly invincible. He was well rounded, and a good role model for me.

I was ordained in May of 1990. Before being ordained I embarked on a job search for my first full-time rabbinic position. To my surprise and joy, Congregation M'kor Shalom in Cherry Hill was on the list of available positions. My heart stopped. The opportunity I had dreamed of was again a possibility. It is not often in our profession that we have the opportunity to work for and with a mentor in our formative years. After a lengthy interview on the phone, we flew to New Jersey for an in-person interview, and the job offer was tendered. I was to begin working for my mentor in July. I felt very fortunate.

The rabbi seemed eager for me to start. He and Carol adopted Debbi and me and our six-month-old son, Ari. We spent our first Rosh Hashanah there having dinner with the rabbi's family. Carol continued to be a guide and confidante to Debbi and me. She guided us through the community, and most importantly, through the congregation. She was honest in sharing insights about members of the congregation, and about the expectations—realistic and unrealistic—that would be placed on us.

Their marriage seemed strong. The rabbi still appeared to like the attention that some women in the congregation paid him, and Carol even joked about it. Yet he seemed devoted to her and their children. Their marriage was a model for us to copy. We didn't realize until much later that there were problems.

I was quickly given more and more responsibility in the synagogue. The rabbi seemed to be pulling back from the day-to-day life of a rapidly growing congregation—as if he were getting tired. I took on more of the "life-cycle" events of the congregation as well as sole responsibility for our confirmation program. Confirmation occurs at the conclusion of the 10th grade when most of the students are 16 years old.

My increased role and the rabbi's seeming withdrawal were not unnoticed by the synagogue leadership. The rabbi was encouraged to take a six-month sabbatical. Sabbaticals are usually used for study in Israel, academic pursuits, or writing books. The rabbi did none of these. He remained in the community, often coming into the building and checking his mail. During this time he grew a ponytail, to the great dismay of the synagogue leadership. There was speculation that he was having a midlife crisis.

He never did fully come back after his sabbatical. I continued with my expanded role and he continued to spend more time away from the office. I never asked what he did with his time, and he never volunteered the information. His kids were getting older and going off to school; their needs were taking more of his time. On the surface, things still seemed fine between him and Carol, although Debbi and I saw them less and less.

As time passed, I began to feel some tension between the rabbi and me. His criticism of my work suddenly increased, which I found perplexing. His moods became volatile. He critiqued sermons as though I had just started the job I had in fact been doing for four years. He seemed to have a need to put me in my place—to make sure I knew that I worked for him. And I felt as though I were carrying too much of a load for an associate rabbi.

I attributed much of this to the fact that during his sabbatical, the congregation—his baby—functioned just fine. I was beginning to develop my own following and perhaps this was not comfortable for him. Whatever the reason, there was tension. It is also possible that I needed to spread my own wings a bit. I was his apprentice, yet I was beginning to have definite ideas of how I wanted things to go. Mentor/student relationships can get complicated when the student feels ready to stand on his or her own.

By September of 1994 I had made the decision that it was time for me to leave M'Kor Shalom. I needed to move away from the rabbi, away from this very large congregation, and toward my own dreams and goals. If someone had stopped and asked about my rabbinic fantasy at that time, I would have said, "Just give me 300 families on Cape Cod and I will be thrilled." I was scheduled to meet with the director of rabbinic placement that December to discuss job possibilities for the coming year.

Life doesn't always work out the way we plan.

CHAPTER 2

# A Terrible Tuesday

As we read through the book of Genesis, we notice that upon completion of each day of creation the Bible states: . . . *and God saw that it was good*. On Tuesday, the third day according to the biblical account, God repeats this phrase twice. Thus, Tuesday has always been considered a lucky day. In many Jewish communities, Tuesdays were historically the preferred days on which to get married.

My appreciation of Tuesdays stopped on November 1, 1994.

That particular Tuesday began with the usual routine: bringing my boys to preschool at the synagogue. Then I traced the familiar path to my office to catch up on paperwork and phone calls, and begin the unpredictable work of a day in the life of a rabbi.

The senior rabbi and I had our weekly meeting, and I went off to prepare for that evening's confirmation class. Throughout their confirmation year, our 16-year-olds study intensely with the rabbi. Their year's work culminates in the service of confirmation, which occurs on the festival of *Shavuot*—the celebration of the day our tradition says God gave the Torah to Moses.

During the 1994-95 calendar year we had a rather large confirmation class. My wife Debbi, also a rabbi, taught one section and I taught the other. That night we were studying Jewish responsibility. The night was not unusual except for the fact that the senior rabbi came to visit my class. He had abdicated confirmation, turning it over to me, and had not dropped in on my class for years. The kids welcomed him warmly and the class continued. How could we have known what was occurring at his home while he sat in our class?

I arrived home about 9:20, took the dog for a walk, changed into pajamas and grabbed a beer from the fridge—my usual Tuesday night routine. As I was preparing to walk into the den to catch *NYPD Blue,* my front door opened. Bob, a member of the synagogue and a dear friend of the rabbi and his family, walked right into my kitchen. No knock, no ring of the bell; he simply walked into my house. I looked at him. His face was ashen; something was definitely wrong.

"Carol is dead!" he said.

"What?" I cried.

He proceeded to tell me they thought it was a robbery, there was a gun—he wasn't sure. But he was sure she was dead. I tried to think of something to say, to be appropriately rabbinic. Nothing came out. I bolted upstairs, got dressed and drove the mile to the rabbi's house.

It was a bitterly cold night. I pulled up to the house, which swarmed with police. They immediately asked me to leave, but I told them who I was and they allowed me to park and enter the murder scene. At that moment, I felt as though I had stepped out of my body and entered some surreal otherworld. The yellow crime scene tape was stretched across the yard. Inside the house I could see detectives dusting the doorways for fingerprints, and the flash of cameras in the living room. Where was the rabbi?

I noticed an ambulance parked in front of the house. I learned that their son, an Emergency Medical Technician, had been driving the ambulance that responded to the emergency call. What must have been going through his mind at that time? I saw his dazed look and approached him. What could I say? What could I do? I embraced him and all he could say was, "I'm worried about my dad." I looked inside the ambulance and there found my friend and mentor, head buried in his hands, sitting in the back of the vehicle. He appeared to be in shock. The ambulance was the only place with heat at that time, so it was a good place for him to be while we tried to comfort him.

Word started spreading through the synagogue community about what had happened. Debbi had called the leadership of the congregation, and they began to arrive. There was chaos, pain, and confusion. I realized I needed to compartmentalize my own fear and shock and take some control over a totally out-of-control situation. I'm a rabbi, with professional responsibilities to comfort my congregants in times of grief. I hugged those who came and said what I could. I knew it wasn't working. There was nothing to say at this time. This was not a situation where someone had suffered a terrible illness and I could say, "She is in a better place." This was a cold-blooded, brutal murder.

The rabbi began to voice concerns that a *vidui* be recited. The *vidui* is the final confession, said upon one's death. A person in a long, slow process of dying can recite the prayer themselves. In this case, someone would need to enter the house, view the bludgeoned body and recite the prayers on Carol's behalf. I knew now what my immediate role would have to be: to educate the police in the Jewish ways of death and mourning; to recite the final confession, the *vidui;* and to help the rabbi and his family prepare for the next few days.

I made sure there were people with the rabbi and his children. His daughter had just arrived from her apartment in Philadelphia. She had no idea what had happened, and I watched helplessly as her terror turned to reality. She held her dad and sobbed. Friends of the family attended to her and her brother. I knew that soon I would have to call the third child, the youngest, and tell him what had occurred.

The rabbi asked me to call the local funeral director and begin making the arrangements. He arrived within minutes, looking as shocked and dumbfounded as anyone there. I began to try educating the police in our ways. I told them that our tradition mandates a speedy burial, usually within 24 to 48 hours. I taught them about shiva, the seven-day period of mourning, which occurs within the house. Could they guarantee that these things would occur in their proper time? I knew the crowds at the funeral would be bigger than anything we had ever seen, so plans needed to be made now. I was told to wait. They understood my concerns and would try to comply—but they were working on a murder here.

By now it was almost midnight. There must have been 40 or 50 friends outside the house. The rabbi and his children were in the warmth of the ambulance, wrapped in blankets. The body was still inside the house. I asked again about *vidui* and funeral arrangements. I was told I could enter the house within the hour. The rabbi asked me to procure his address book from inside the house and call his youngest son, a freshman at a Midwestern university. The police told me they would give me the address book as soon as they could.

Two AM: we were still out in the cold. Finally, there was a signal from inside to bring me into the house. I was torn by my emotions. First there was relief that this surreal experience was coming to some sort of closure. Then terror overtook me as I moved up the walk and headed into the foyer. As I placed one foot in the doorway, I saw black fingerprinting dust all over the house. Then I glimpsed Carol's legs in the living room; then a huge pool of blood on the white rug. They didn't let me go any further. "Wait outside," I was told. "We will bring her to you." Perhaps they saw the terror in my face.

I stepped outside and waited for what seemed an eternity. Fifteen minutes later, two police officers approached carrying a large, black zippered body bag. I had only seen such a sight before on television. They placed Carol gently on the ground beside me. They suggested I not unzip the bag. With tears in my eyes and a huge lump in my throat I recited the words of the *vidui:*

> *My God and God of my ancestors, may my prayers reach up to you. Forgive me for all my sins which I have sinned before you from the time of my birth until this time. . . . If only my hands were clean and my heart pure! Protector of the bereaved and the helpless, watch over my loved ones. Into your hand I commit my spirit; redeem it, O God of mercy and truth.*

Then, I recited the words of the memorial prayer, *El malei rachamim:*

> *God, full of compassion, grant perfect rest in your sheltering presence to Carol, who has entered eternity. God of mercy, let her find refuge in your eternal presence and let her soul be bound up in the bond of everlasting life. God is her inheritance. May she rest in peace.*

With that, Carol was taken away.

It was now close to 3:00 AM and I had not yet retrieved the rabbi's phone book from the house. The rabbi and his children had been taken down to the police station for questioning. Robbery still seemed to be the motive, yet it was clear by now that no gun had been involved. Carol had been brutally bludgeoned to death. I finally located the phone number I was looking for. The cantor and I took an agonizingly long drive to the synagogue to call the youngest son, and tell him his mother had just been murdered.

How could I place this call? What could I say? I decided I did not want him to be alone when he heard what I had to tell him. I found the phone number for the local Hillel rabbi in the son's area, woke him up, and told him what was happening. I asked him to go to the apartment, sit with the son, and wait for my call. That bought me 15 minutes to compose myself and prepare for the most difficult phone call of my life.

I placed the call; their son answered. I gave him the terrible news, knowing that he stopped listening to me after the first sentence. He asked what had happened and I tried to tell him. I told him his dad and brother and sister were OK and would call him soon. There was no response. I told him I loved him and I would help him through every minute of the next few weeks. The rabbi out there took the phone. He said he would take over on his end.

At that moment all my rabbinic training felt utterly, totally useless.

CHAPTER 3

# Dark Clouds, Burning Flames

The next 48 hours were a blur. At some point I went down to the police station to check in on the family, to see what I could do. It didn't seem right that they had just experienced the murder of their wife and mother, yet they could not grieve. They were being interrogated individually in the cold, dark confines of the police station. Eventually the family was able to leave, but they could not return to their home. They moved in with dear friends down the street.

I arrived home at 5:00 AM, hugged my wife, cried, and began to think of all that needed to be done. What to do now? Where to start? How to take care of my rabbi and his family? How to take care of my congregation when I was in shock and grieving myself?

Endless questions; no answers.

The news began to hit the airwaves around 7:00 AM. I had forgotten that no one in the general community had any idea of what had happened. The early headlines simply said, "Rabbi's wife killed in Old Orchard neighborhood in Cherry Hill." Our phone began ringing off the hook. We lived in the Old Orchard neighborhood as well. Our friends were hysterical, thinking that Debbi might be dead. We assured them that Debbi was fine—but then we had to tell them that Carol was dead.

*Carol was dead.*

I had yet to deal with that. Then reporters began calling, wanting a reaction from the synagogue and me. I had no way of knowing this was just the opening of the floodgates, and that I would soon have more contact with media representatives than I would ever have dreamed—or wanted. Some were sensitive and intelligent, and earned my respect. Some were intolerably aggressive and callous; those I came to despise.

I knew we needed to say something. I also knew my congregation was heading into as traumatic a period as a religious community can experience. I phoned the president of the synagogue and arranged for all the leaders and staff members to meet at 8:30 AM to plan the next 48 hours.

We met in the rabbi's office. We began by holding hands, shedding tears and offering a memorial prayer for Carol. We then joined in the words of the Kaddish—the traditional prayer a mourner says after suffering a personal loss. *May the God who grants peace in the heavens above grant peace to all Israel and all humankind.* Those present responded with a hushed "Amen."

What should we do? Streams of people were already coming to the synagogue because they didn't know where else to go. I realized this would probably go on all day. Although it was not in accord with Jewish tradition, we made the decision to hold a community memorial service that evening. We got word out through the synagogue office and through the media. Since this was the top news story, we used that to our advantage to spread the word of arrangements for the service. I called the rabbi, told him why I felt we needed to do this, and assured him he need not be there if he felt it would be too much for him.

Tears, hugs and disbelief poured from all who came by. Comforting my congregants, while difficult, was not the most painful thing I had to do on November 2, 1994. I had arranged to meet the rabbi back at his home. He and I, the funeral director, and the local director of our Jewish Community Center—a good friend of the rabbi—would enter the home together. The police had secured it for 18 hours but had now released it back to its rightful owner.

How would we prepare this home for the seven-day period of shiva? How would we deal with the images that are engraved in my mind to this day? Carol was killed in the living room of their four-bedroom colonial house. The living room featured a beautiful white carpet—now grotesquely soiled by a three-foot bloodstain. I could picture Carol lying in that awful pool of blood. Then I looked around the room. Blood was everywhere. There were bloodstains on the wallpaper, the window shades, even near the ceiling. There was clearly a struggle. Carol had fought hard.

But why the rage? I'm no murder expert; but I wondered, why not a gun? Why the rage of brutally beating someone to death? Did this person know her? What could she have done to make someone so angry? It just didn't make any sense.

Still, the room had to be cleaned and the house prepared. I watched the rabbi, clearly in a fog, walk through the room and show the maintenance man who had just arrived where to clean, where to paint, how to take up the carpet. No one should ever have to do what the rabbi was doing, I thought. Yet he showed what appeared to be courage in handling this unbelievable situation.

Memories of that room haunted me, troubling my sleep for weeks.

We finally left the rabbi's house and went to the home where he and his children had been staying. A rabbinic colleague from Philadelphia, a long-time friend of the rabbi, would officiate at the funeral with me. The two of us sat with bewildered children and our despondent friend, talking about the details of what would happen tomorrow. It occurred to me that the rabbi, a man who had officiated at close to a thousand funerals, was totally lost and distracted. He couldn't follow what we were saying.

We talked about Carol. Each of the kids shared the beauty of the memories they held dear. We took notes, trying to determine how we would weave them into a tapestry of Carol's life.

That day that I began a very special friendship, one that continues to this day, with Carol's siblings—particularly with one of her brothers and his wife. Their pain was profound. Their grief was compounded by the fact that they could not see her to say goodbye. Due to the viciousness of the murder, no one from the family was permitted to view her one last time. They felt helplessness and pain in imagining the last things she saw and felt in this life, and the horror of her death. There was also a large dose of confusion. The story of the robbery just didn't sit right with them. Even then, they thought there must be more to this than met the eye.

Traditional Jewish ritual calls for funeral services to be held at the gravesite or a funeral home. But we decided we would have Carol's funeral in the synagogue—something this congregation had never done before. Carol warranted such an honor. We took leave of our friends and I began to prepare for that evening.

By 7:30 PM, a thousand individuals had filled the sanctuary. There was a hush; yet I sensed an atmosphere of shock in the silence that filled the room. I was locked away in my office trying to find the strength to stand before my congregation and help them through their confusion, while I was paralyzed by my own.

My thoughts turned to memories of Carol. She was a strong-willed woman with a heart of gold. She was candid, honest: she "told it like it was." Carol was also a wonderful confidante. She had a unique ability to read people and offer guidance. She was enormously helpful to Debbi and me as we worked on the difficult balancing act between our own personal and family needs, and the needs of the congregation. I think in many ways Carol's resentment of the congregation and the time it took away from her family stemmed from the fact that it had grown so large so fast. It was truly overwhelming to manage.

My thoughts drifted back to happier times—the visit in Israel . . .

I could wait no longer. I made the seemingly endless walk to the sanctuary.

We began with the cantor singing a song that would become our anthem for the next two years. *Makom she libi ohev . . . the place that my heart holds dear, my feet will bring me there.* The words of this song clearly resonated within the hearts and souls of those in attendance. I stepped up to the podium, trying to find my voice amidst the lump in my throat.

> *Friends, we gather here in the protective shelter of God's healing love. We are free to pour out our grief, release our anger, face our emptiness, and know that God cares.*
> *We gather here as God's people, conscious of others who have died and the frailty of our own existence on earth.*
> *We come to comfort and support one another in our common loss. We gather to hear God's word of hope that can drive away our despair and move us to offer God our praise.*

After reading that prayer from the United Church of Christ pastor's manual, I looked out into the eyes of my congregation. "We should not be here," I said. "This is not how our world is supposed to work."

We then listened to the cantor chant the haunting melody of the 23rd Psalm. All present joined in the translation. They imbued it with a power beyond anything I had heard from this congregation before. There was silence, more prayers, more music. The cantor and I did our best to voice the grief of our congregation. ("When do *we* get to grieve?" I wondered, perhaps selfishly. "When do *we* get to fall apart?")

I had found a prayer in our synagogue prayer book which did not have attribution. Its words seemed particularly fitting for the moment:

> *Here, in the dark valley of my sorrow, I am alone.*
> *Alone with new fears, alone with longing regrets, alone with questions. Why? Why? O God, enter this isolation.*
> *Open me to my friends, soften me to receive the caring of*

*those who reach out. Surround my grief. Wrap me in your brightness. Turn my heart to you. Help me, even now, to trust in your peace. Open my lips, that my mouth may declare your praise.*

After the memorial prayer and another singing of our "anthem," we moved into the first phase of formalized congregational grief work. Graciously, almost a dozen rabbinic colleagues and therapists had attended the service and agreed to counsel breakout groups at its conclusion. Many of the congregants chose to take advantage of this opportunity to talk to a sympathetic ear. Others were overwhelmed with the numbness of shock and disbelief. How could this happen to someone I know? How could this happen in peaceful Cherry Hill, NJ? Why would anyone want to kill Carol? Most of us had only heard initial reports that the murder was related to her business; that she had carried home large sums of money and was followed and killed.

Many felt pure, concentrated fear. They lived in similar neighborhoods. Their doors were usually not locked when they were home. "That could have been me!" was a familiar refrain. People grappled with how to talk to their kids about the murder. Most had spoken with their children about death; many had endured the death of a loved one. But few had ever had to teach their children about the horror of death by murder. We realized that night, as the discussions began, that we had all been victimized.

There is a spiritual dynamic to murder that I had never had any reason to think about before. Each of us lives with hopes and expectations of how our lives will progress. We create dreams and visions of a future filled with joys and blessings. These images are vital: they give our spirit strength to survive and goals to work for. We *have* to live believing our marriages will last, our kids will grow up healthy, we'll be blessed with grandchildren, we'll live out our days in peace and bliss. Carol's murder rocked that foundation. Now, everything was in question. We wondered if we would wake up the next morning. We feared future tragedies. The universe suddenly blasted our lives with a perilous show of chaos, violence and uncertainty. Our foundation had crumbled, leaving us churning in a rubble of grief and pain.

Questions of our faith arose. How does God permit such atrocities to occur? Does God really watch over and protect us? I answered as best I could. Over and over, I shared my theological perspective of a God who loves us, a God who created us with certain fundamental rights. To be human is to have dominion over our lives. To be human is to have the power to discern between good and evil. "God did not create evil," I told them. God created humanity and humanity creates evil. For God to intervene and reshape the pattern of our lives—to change the decisions we make—would deny us our fundamental humanity.

Rabbi Harold Kushner paints an evocative image of a God who sits and weeps at the decisions God's creations make. "We need to draw strength from God," I said. People were far too emotionally raw and vulnerable to delve into deep philosophical discussions. But I knew that eventually, both privately and from the pulpit, I would need to come up with much deeper wisdom and understanding to deal with the massive spiritual crisis we were going through.

Next morning, November 3, was the funeral. The arrangements were made and I arrived at the synagogue early. I struggled to prepare for the service. Thankfully, my rabbinic colleague from Philadelphia would deliver the formal eulogy. But I knew that leading the service would be no easy task.

I remember sitting in my office, feeling as though I were living in a movie. I had flashbacks to Tuesday night, and wasn't sure if I was remembering reality or an *NYPD Blue* episode. Over the next few months that feeling of reality blurring would become an all-too-frequent and unwelcome visitor.

The funeral director arrived first—a gentle giant of a man, a true mensch, clearly dealing with his own grief and shock as he tried to comfort those around him. Debbi, the cantor and I walked into the sanctuary. No one was there—but Carol. Her plain, traditional pine-box coffin, draped with a Jewish star, now filled the aisle in front of the *bima,* the raised platform upon which services are led. The image was haunting and painful. Each of us touched the casket, held each other and cried.

I still couldn't accept it. I wanted desperately to believe that this was a dream. I felt so inadequate to be the one my congregation was turning to for comfort and strength when I was in such pain myself. I thanked God privately for my wife and family. I thought of Debbi, four months pregnant. How did we deserve such blessing in our life while Carol's family was in agony? Again the memories, the holiday dinners, the insightful conversations I had with Carol came back. I was as deeply saddened at that moment as any other time I could remember. I suddenly realized that this might be my only opportunity of the day to really feel my own loss and pain.

In that powerful moment Debbi and I shared grief, yet drew strength from each other.

The crowds began to form. The rabbi, his family, Carol's family and the congregational family started entering the sanctuary. I learned later from the evening news that the crowd swelled above 2,000 and the receiving line stretched half a mile up the road. Eventually, we had to cut off the traditional receiving line; it was clearly too much for the family. It was time to begin.

We started, as we always do, by asking the family to rise. The rabbi, his children and Carol's siblings were wearing black ribbons on their outer garments. We made a tear on the ribbon, symbolizing the tear at the core of their souls. I explained that they didn't need an outward sign of grief. This ribbon, a universal symbol of mourning, conveyed the message. They sat down and we began the service.

Carol had a favorite reading from our prayer book, a reading that spoke of the need for faith and strength in a world broken and needing repair. I shared that reading:

> *We cannot merely pray to you, O God, to end war; for we know that you have made the world in a way that we must find our own path to peace within ourselves and with our neighbors.*
>
> *We cannot merely pray to you, O God, to end starvation; for you have already given us the resources to feed the entire world, if we would only use them wisely.*
>
> *We cannot merely pray to you, O God, to root out prejudice; for you have already given us eyes with which to see the good in everyone, if we would only use them rightly.*
>
> *We cannot merely pray to you, O God, to end despair; for you have already given us the power to clear away slums*

*and to give hope to the needy, if we would only use our power justly.*

*We cannot merely pray to you, O God, to end disease; for you have already given us great minds with which to search out cures and healings, if we would only use them constructively.*

*We cannot merely pray to you, O God, to eradicate ignorance; for you have already given us light to illumine the pathways of darkness, if we would only use our minds and hearts to the full.*

*Therefore, we pray to you instead, O God, for strength, determination and willpower, to do instead of just to pray, to become instead of merely to wish.*

*For your sake and for ours, speedily and soon, that our world may be safe and that our lives may be blessed.*

*May the words that we pray, and the deeds that we do be acceptable before you, O God, our rock and our redeemer.*

As I concluded the reading, I looked around the room. The faces reflected the same dazed, perplexed look I had been seeing in my mirror the past two days. How could we be here? How could this have happened? Two thousand people. Members of this congregation, members of the local clergy, politicians and dignitaries. All in mourning; all in shock.

Tears appeared as the cantor again sang the 23rd Psalm. We shared the translation. My Philadelphia colleague then delivered a beautiful and touching eulogy. People there learned things they had never known about Carol. He spoke of the beauty of her life, and the lives she had touched in her too few years on this earth.

When it was my turn, I faced her children and reminded them how proud she had been of them and their accomplishments. I shared my own memories of moments spent with her: time in Israel together; the valuable advice she offered me and Debbi about living as rabbis and rabbi's spouses; Rosh Hashanah meals shared in their home. Then I gave the congregation time to reflect on their own memories of Carol.

The cantor then led us in the memorial prayer—the same prayer I had said while standing beside the black zippered bag holding Carol's body the night of the murder. We read the translation and concluded the service. Pallbearers were called to escort the casket from the sanctuary to the hearse. As we exited the synagogue we were greeted by the hovering throngs of media who had set up camp on the synagogue lawn opposite the limousines. Somehow their presence violated the sanctity and privacy of the moment. It didn't enter my mind that this was the biggest news story breaking in the greater Philadelphia area. I didn't focus on the unsolved mystery of her death, or the rumors sweeping the airwaves. Our Carol was dead. Our community had suffered a deep and tragic loss. That was my focus.

I drove my car right behind the family limousine. The rabbi from Philadelphia, his wife and my wife were in the car with me, and we all sensed the nightmarish quality of the events swirling around us. At each intersection, local and state police assured clear passage on the 10-mile journey to the cemetery. There must have been 300 people at the grave as we recited psalms, lowered the casket and filled the grave.

Carol had been buried, but the pain and anguish were just beginning to set in. There were still so many unanswered questions. It was now time for the seven days of shiva. Judaism teaches us that these days are a time for reflection and remembering. They offered us a time to recall how Carol had touched our lives. Shiva took place at the Neulander home. The living room had been completely redone and was ready for visitors.

That evening I arrived at the house for the daily service done at a shiva home, including appropriate memorial prayers. I couldn't bear to look into the living room, remembering what I had last seen there. It amazed me how that night, and each night after, the rabbi sat in the very room in which his wife had been killed. I was both awed by his strength and confused by his insistence on spending time in that room. Hundreds of people came to the home to pay their respects and attend the shiva service. This scene was repeated throughout the week.

At the synagogue, we organized time for the children in the religious schools to meet with counselors and share their feelings and fears. This was their first encounter with murder. Since the murder was reported to be a random act of violence—a robbery gone bad—the kids were afraid for their own safety and that of their parents. It was our hope that the synagogue could be a safe place for the children to express their emotions.

Weeks passed. The pain diminished to a persistent dull ache for some, but only increased for others. In Judaic practice, as the week of shiva concludes and the 30 days of mourning called *shloshim* move forward, we slowly make our way back into the world. One beautiful thing that occurred during this time was the formation of a daily minyan (a morning prayer service) at the synagogue. We had never had such a service, but we felt our rabbi should not have to attend a different and more traditional synagogue to say the Kaddish, the daily prayer for mourners. We took turns leading the service. I remember vividly that on Thanksgiving Day the small chapel was filled with nearly a hundred people in a show of support for our rabbi.

The daily minyan service was very meaningful for me. It was cathartic as well as spiritually powerful. It offered structure for processing the grief and the chaos I felt. It continues to this day as a Sunday morning service.

December brought increasing confusion. The police began questioning me and those around me the Friday after the funeral. They said this was simply standard operating procedure in a murder case. The questions sounded anything but standard. They were probing hard about the Neulanders' marriage and the rabbi's personal life.

Each time they called or stopped by the synagogue, my stomach knotted up. I had never had much contact with detectives before, and certainly never with homicide detectives. They didn't belong in the synagogue! We needed to reclaim the synagogue as a holy place. Yet day after day it seemed anything but holy, due in large part to the continued police presence. I felt as though the detectives were watching me. I even became somewhat paranoid that they might regard me or one of my coworkers as a suspect in the crime.

The constant stream of badge-bearing investigators was an excruciating intrusion into our mourning process.

They were relentless. They caught me coming to my office, tracked me to my home, followed Debbi and me as we went out for lunch. Once we emerged from a restaurant and, to our surprise, were met by two detectives we had started to call "Starsky and Hutch." They employed techniques we thought only existed on TV. One would comment on the books or toys in my office and try to make me comfortable. Then the other would ask me a question about the rabbi's personal life or some other equally out-of-the-blue topic. These were just part of the continual reminders that I was now part of a murder mystery.

The anger that raged within me toward the police was exceeded by what I felt toward the prosecutor's office. There was no respect for me as a rabbi, or for the synagogue and our need to heal. They began to share unwanted details of the rabbi's personal life. They also began trying to isolate him from the rest of us. They made it clear that their investigation showed Carol's murder was not a random act of violence, but a carefully planned "hit." This seemed implausible; who would want to kill Carol? The investigators had their ideas, which they were only too happy to share with those of us close to the rabbi.

Their tactics to isolate the rabbi worked. I grew unsure about whether I could trust him. I felt I needed to talk to him before giving my formal statement at police headquarters, and approached him the day before I was to testify. The rabbi told me where he thought the investigation was going and some of the questions they might ask. He then confided details of his personal life that he knew would be revealed to me the next day by the police. He asked for clergy/penitent confidentiality with regard to this information, which put me in a stressful situation. I would have to withhold information from the authorities.

They would want what I knew and I would not—*could* not—share it with them.

I walked into that interrogation as nervous as I have ever been. I felt positive that someone was watching me through a one-way mirror in the back of the room and that everything I said would be twisted. I asked if I needed a lawyer. The police responded, "Have you done anything wrong?" They kept me almost two hours with question after question about Carol, the rabbi, their relationship and the synagogue. They asked questions I couldn't answer because I wouldn't break the rabbi's confidence. They knew I was holding something back. They also knew I wasn't going to share it with them. They tried to instill trust, assuring me that whatever I told them would be held in the strictest confidence. I felt as though they suspected I was in some sort of collusion with the rabbi. About what, I wasn't sure.

I had never pictured a life scenario that would lead me to a police interrogation room. When our little session was over I felt physically ill.

I never did fully trust the officials working the case. My gut told me to keep my guard up. Sure enough, the next morning I read pieces of information in the newspaper that could only have come from my interrogation. The prosecutor had leaked my testimony in an attempt to flush out other information. Infuriated, I called the prosecutor directly and we set up a clandestine late-evening meeting in a local diner. A secret meeting with the DA's office! Now it really felt like I was in a movie. He assured me the synagogue's interests would be protected. The next day he issued a statement decrying the leaks from his department.

The investigators used tactics I considered to be unethical, but I realized that they spend a lot of time dealing with unethical human beings. Maybe sometimes you do have to fight fire with fire. I'm sure theirs was not an easy job.

Even more intrusive and more unethical were some of the media. Over time I learned more about how to deal with the media—and unfortunately, I also learned to despise many members of the profession. From the very first moment of this crisis, the media intruded on the sacred space of the synagogue and interfered in the healing process. Their phone calls came to the office, to my home and to the homes of congregants. They stationed themselves outside the local deli and asked questions relating to the gossip swirling around the community. They showed little regard for the fact that we were real human beings dealing with complex emotions.

One reporter earned our trust: a Jewish woman from the major Philadelphia newspaper. She was the only one who showed any respect for what we were going through. She honored my desire not to be quoted, understanding that it was difficult for my congregants to have to read about both their rabbis in the news. Some three years later, she became the first reporter I willingly sat down with to share my thoughts. She recognized the value of avoiding gossip, and she understood the aims of the synagogue.

I was most disillusioned by the Philadelphia Jewish press. Their lead reporter's treatment of us seemed the most invasive and insensitive of the bunch. She acted as if she felt that because she was also Jewish, I owed her information I wouldn't share with others. She repeatedly called my home, tracked me down on vacations, and continued to publish stories about the murder and the investigation which I felt contained elements of malicious gossip. I learned much about the seamy side of human nature from unscrupulous reporters, the side that panders to the public's yen for juicy gossip and unsavory tidbits that are really no one else's business.

As the police increased their pressure and continued to intrude upon the sanctity of the synagogue, rumors swirled faster. The investigation seemed to be moving away from the original robbery theory and into new, disturbing directions. The push for information on the rabbi's personal life grew more concerted. I tried to educate the officials about the Jewish view of rumor, gossip and innuendo. We call this *lashon hara:* evil talk.

By December, 1994, rumors had become so commonplace that I felt I had to deal with the topic of *lashon hara* from the pulpit. One Friday evening during services, I shared a true and troubling story with the congregation. I had been out to lunch with a friend in a popular local restaurant and overheard the conversation at the table behind us. The people at that table were talking about the rabbi and rumors they had heard. Then the discussion turned to me. One said she had heard I was seen at a restaurant with a woman other than my wife. The second responded that all rabbis were flirtatious and inclined toward extramarital encounters. I was shocked, but not surprised. As I left, I walked over to their table and very quietly dropped one of my business cards before the two women. "You never know who might be behind you," I said.

Their faces turned pale. They looked like they wanted to apologize. But they were so shocked and mortified that nothing could come out of their mouths.

I then told the congregation one of my favorite stories from Jewish lore—a story I would tell many times over the next three years because of its powerful point regarding the damage of gossip.

> A young man in a certain village maliciously spread gossip about another in the village. Soon after the incident, the man regretted what he had said and went to his rabbi for advice on how to make right the wrong that he had committed.
>
> The rabbi sent him on a task. He told the man to fill a pillowcase with feathers and walk around to each door of every home in the village and place a feather on the steps in front of the door. The man did not understand how this would make him feel better, but he listened and obliged the rabbi. After he had finished he came back to the rabbi. "I did as you asked, but I do not feel any better, nor do I understand the purpose of this task," stated the man.
>
> The rabbi told him he was not yet done with the task. Then he told the man to go back to each home and gather up the feathers and place them back in the bag. The man did as the rabbi said, but soon became very frustrated: as he approached each home, he found the feather was no longer there. The wind had blown it away. He came back with an empty bag and told the rabbi the feathers were nowhere to be found.
>
> "Good," said the rabbi. "Now you have learned the lesson. You see, words are like those feathers. When you

> misuse words and repeat gossip, it spreads and flies through the community like those feathers. The words can never be taken back, just as the feathers cannot be collected." With that, the man realized he could not undo what he had done. He could only resolve to never again spread rumors or gossip.

I concluded that night by stating that evil talking is sometimes worse than evil doing. Gossip, once started, cannot be stopped. Words can be swords, inflicting deadly pain. With that, I implored my congregation not to participate in the ugliness of the gossip that had pervaded our community. I urged that the synagogue be a safe place—a place free from hurtful words and *lashon hara*.

Over the next few years, I offered that sermon whenever I felt we needed to revisit this difficult topic. I believe that in some small way it did contribute to a lessening of the talk within the synagogue. I was not so naive as to think it would have an impact beyond the walls of our building and the homes of our members.

What I could not share with the congregation was my own inner pain and struggle. I had come to this synagogue to work with my mentor. I had had other wonderful opportunities and turned them down for this chance. I needed "my" rabbi and I was losing him. I also needed to grieve and didn't feel I had an opportunity to do so, because I had to focus on shepherding the congregation through our communal nightmare.

I felt grossly inadequate for the task. Leading a congregation of this size was a responsibility which, in the normal course of events, would cap a career 20 years longer than mine had been so far.

Thanks to the investigators, the rabbi, and my position in the synagogue, I was now privy to more information about the murder and the rabbi's private life than I ever wanted to know. I churned with inner conflict regarding my mentor. I was angry for being put in a position to have to guard information; and I was guilty for being angry with someone who had just tragically lost his wife.

On a very selfish note, I felt that my own life was in complete upheaval. Two months prior to the murder, I had made the decision to leave the synagogue the following June. It was time to fly away from the safety and sheltered life of an associate rabbi and pursue my dream of leading a smaller congregation. I had updated my résumé and contacted the rabbinic placement office. Debbi was pregnant, and our new baby was due in April. She needed me. My kids needed me. They were beginning to question why Daddy was never home anymore, and Debbi had to take permanent leave from her job to be with them. I was no longer a reliable husband or father, and I felt totally unequipped to lead the synagogue rabbinically. As I told my mentor one day, I didn't know whether to hug him or slug him.

Now my personal dreams and goals would have to wait. Not for a minute, however, did I anticipate they would have to wait five more years.

I was plagued with nightmares of the murder scene: the entryway of the house as Carol's body was brought out; her legs and the large pool of blood in the living room; the horror of the crime scene as we tried to prepare the house for shiva. These terrifyingly vivid images would not leave. A therapist friend suggested a special kind of visual imagery to help me erase the scenes from my mind. She had me picture a safe place and learn to replace the painful images with visions of my sacred, safe space. It helped tremendously.

By January of 1995, rumors of the rabbi's adultery hit the media. The rabbi took a leave of absence from the synagogue to sort through his own grief and the reality of his ethical breaches. The synagogue's board met weekly, sometimes twice a week, to deal with the situation. I emphasized over and over that we had to be sure we were not participating in the gossip loop. The synagogue needed to be a safe place, a place that upheld the morals and teachings of our tradition. The synagogue could not be the vehicle for satisfying people's curiosity and intrigue. I urged them to take the ethical high road and not give in to pressure to reveal any of the sordid details of rabbinic indiscretion. We decided on a policy of not sharing any information—true or otherwise—with members of the congregation or the media.

By mid-February of 1995, a supposed leak from the office of the Camden County Prosecutor named the rabbi as a suspect in the murder of his wife. It is standard investigative procedure in any murder to consider the husband or wife a potential suspect, but this unfortunate rumor clouded issues for the synagogue. The rabbi's leave of absence had nothing whatever to do with these new allegations about the murder. Convincing the congregation and the community of this would be another matter.

Friday, February 24th would be a day to remember. There had been meetings between synagogue leadership, the regional director of the Philadelphia area Reform movement, and the rabbi. Their discussions ultimately helped the rabbi make the only decision that had a chance to preserve some sense of his integrity. He needed to resign his position. An emergency board meeting was necessary to formalize the resignation, but we were about to enter into the Sabbath at sundown.

We decided that this was simply too important in the life of the congregation and it couldn't wait. We called an emergency meeting for right after services at the home of one of the vice-presidents. The cantor, president and I were the only ones who knew what was happening.

At the meeting, the president wasted no time sharing the news with the board of directors: the rabbi had resigned. Even though I knew it was coming, those words hit me like a ton of bricks. It occurred to me at that moment that although I had been functioning alone as rabbi for three months, now I was truly, *formally* alone in that position. And we were without our founding rabbi.

There was a gasp, some tears, and then we dug in for a heartfelt and productive dialogue.

We spent hours trying to figure out how to break the news to the congregation. Many members were growing angry with the lack of information from the leadership. I continued to preach that we should take the ethical high road. I did not want this synagogue to spread the continuing rumors—true or false. Yes, sharing the truth in full detail would take us off the hook and make it easier for everyone to accept the resignation. However, I believed strongly that was not the Jewish thing to do.

Ultimately, the board agreed. We would try to hold the meeting in a spiritual, honest way, but we would avoid any rumor, gossip or sharing of unnecessary information.

It was not the job of the synagogue to reveal the dirt of this tragic tale.

The day arrived: Sunday, February 26th. The sanctuary was filled to capacity with people waiting to hear an explanation of the rabbi's leave of absence, and how we were going to address congregational discontent. We began, as we did throughout this crisis, with music. I led an opening prayer. Then the president of the congregation read her bombshell: the letter from the rabbi announcing his resignation.

Gasps filled the room. This was not what people were expecting to hear. Many rose and expressed anger that the synagogue would accept a resignation from a rabbi who had done so much for his community. Some were outraged, and accused the synagogue of giving in to the rumors.

We had made the conscious decision not to release what we now knew to be facts, not rumors, about the rabbi's personal life. People might hear them—but they would not hear them from us. Those facts, as the rabbi himself realized, absolutely and unambiguously disqualified him from the office of senior rabbi. Our dilemma was that telling those facts was counter to our ethics. And not telling them left the congregation feeling there wasn't adequate reason for them to be losing their founding rabbi.

There were tears, there was shouting, there was the pain of the rabbi's own son at the microphone. The meeting adjourned after an hour. The controversy and anguish were just starting.

The rabbi's resignation made headlines, and the rumored details of his personal life emerged as factual public information in the pages of the newspapers. I could only hope that those who had expressed their frustration with us the previous Sunday morning would now understand the service we were trying to do for the rabbi by not telling them everything we knew. It would have been so easy to simply reveal the truth and let the facts speak for themselves. I truly believe that the way the synagogue leadership handled this aspect of the crisis allowed us to emerge with a sense of dignity in a very undignified situation.

We were still in mourning for Carol, and we had just lost our spiritual leader. I was 31 years old and now the acting—the only—rabbi of the congregation. I felt as if I were trying to ride a cyclone, at the mercy of events beyond control, but dictating my every move. I needed to get grounded myself before I could help the congregation heal from a tragedy that kept growing.

And that help needed to start at our next Friday evening service. What could I possibly say? How could we best deal with the many layers of this tragedy? Looking at the weekly portion from the Torah prescribed for reading that Sabbath, I gave the following sermon for our March 3, 1995 service:

> This has been a week of confusion, bewilderment and grief. This has been a week where the foundation of this synagogue has been shaken; however, it *did* not and *will* not crumble. It is appropriate that this week we conclude perhaps the most dramatic book of the Bible, the book of Exodus. We conclude with a story of building and hope. We conclude with a story about the ever-presence of God

in our lives as a source of strength. We conclude Exodus with the knowledge that God is our foundation and we, God's children, can overcome tremendous challenges.

In this week's Torah portion, the people of Israel put the finishing touches on the Tabernacle, the portable synagogue that would accompany the Israelites on their journey through the desert. Moses actually had to tell the people to stop giving of their gold, silver and gems; they gave more than was necessary to complete the structure. (This past week, our nominating committee nominated Moses to be our next fundraiser.) The people built that first synagogue with dedication, love and whatever means was available. They invested all they had in their synagogue.

This synagogue is no different. Fred Neulander and a small group of dedicated souls built this place and gave it purpose. Through the years there were new faces, new visions and new mortar and bricks. The purpose of M'kor Shalom, the family of families, remained. This place became the most vibrant, innovative force in our area due to the creativity, dedication and vision of not one individual, but many. This tabernacle, this holy space, stands strong and together because we are bound by a common purpose and a common heritage of mercy, compassion and justice. We are bound by our teachings, values and relationship with God.

We are told in this week's portion that *When Moses had finished the work, the cloud covered the tent of meeting, and the presence of the Lord filled the tabernacle. Moses could not enter the tent of meeting because the cloud had settled upon it and the presence of the Lord filled the tabernacle.* (Exodus 40:33-35)

My friends, the cloud that covered the first tabernacle was a sign that God was with the people. It was a cloud of God's protection and love. The cloud gave the people strength.

Many of us have felt and may continue to feel that there is a cloud hanging over our tabernacle, a dark cloud over M'kor Shalom; a cloud that somehow tells others that this place is not the place to enter; a cloud of suspicion; a cloud of intrigue. We must learn from this week's Torah portion.

It is our job to take control of that cloud and see it and have it seen for what it is. *There is no dark cloud over our spiritual home.* This is a place to be proud of. This is a place to be cherished. This is a special place, a holy place. The only cloud that covers our synagogue is the cloud of the presence of God: a cloud that has given our people strength to overcome adversity and meet life's greatest challenges.

It is a cliché to say there is a lining of silver in each and every cloud. That is not true for our cloud. Our cloud is lined with *gold*. The people who lead this synagogue are as precious as gold. Through the trials and tribulations of the last weeks, our synagogue leadership has conducted itself with integrity, dignity and grace. They have given hours and hours to helping this synagogue and Rabbi Neulander through this crisis. The discussions occurred on the highest ethical plane and the decisions arrived at were ones made with the utmost of sensitivity and compassion.

In short, the gold that lines our cloud has been guided by Jewish ideals and values. The media feeding frenzy was quelled and the honor and dignity of my friend, our teacher and guide was preserved. If this does not send a message to our Jewish community and to the community at large that this is a special place—a holy place—I don't know what will. We could not ask for better, stronger or more capable leaders; we owe them a great deal.

The gold that lies within this cloud is also due to Rabbi Neulander. His vision, his creativity and dedication helped guide and shape this synagogue. The gold is found in the times he touched our lives. The gold is found in the sacred moments of time shared with him along the path of life, each stage of the life cycle made holy with his help. We owe him an eternal debt of gratitude for all he did for us these past 20 years. Our hearts ache for him, and for us. We pray that he finds the strength to overcome his pain and move forward, again having the opportunity to touch lives and uplift souls. We pray that we find the strength to draw on what he taught us for so many years, the strength to move forward. We pray for the strength to take ownership of the cloud, the cloud of God's protection and love.

We are told at the very end of this week's portion that when the cloud was not covering the tabernacle, a fire—another powerful representation of God—was visible in the midst of the Sanctuary. We must look within the flames that seem to surround our life and find the presence of God as well. We can take our cue from Moses.

When Moses first met God it was through the flames of a bush that burned but was not consumed by the flames. Moses happened upon this sight in the desert. Moses quickly turned aside to see this great sight. When God saw that Moses turned to look, God called to Moses "out of the midst of the bush."

Perhaps what made Moses the greatest of prophets is that he not only saw God in the midst of the physical flames of the bush, but also in the midst of the personal flames of his life. Remember the difficulties that Moses had encountered in just three short chapters of the Bible. He's born in an apple orchard; his mother hides him for three months and sends him down the river in a basket. He grows up in a strange Egyptian home. He sees a taskmaster kill a slave, so he kills the Egyptian and flees his adoptive family. Tired, scared and alone, he confronts the flames and finds God.

We have all had difficulties in our lives. We have all had to wrestle with personal flames and disasters. As a community we have experienced the flames of loss, anger and confusion during the past weeks. The beauty of the Moses narrative is that we learn that if we look deeply enough into these flames of our lives we can find God, and therefore strength and comfort.

The flames that burn within our lives are the flames of our faith. The eternal flame that glows above the ark tells us God is near. The flames of justice and mercy that burned within the prophets burn within us as well. These flames compel us to move forward and to better our world. These are the flames that compel us to fight injustice and hatred; the flames that teach us to clothe the needy and feed the hungry and house the homeless. These are the flames of Judaism. This is what kindles our spirit and gives us purpose. This is what we have been taught from this pulpit and what we in turn teach our children: that we can make a difference; that Judaism can give us a blueprint to change the world.

So we move forward. We move forward with purpose, meaning and integrity. We look back at what we have been taught by the Torah, by Rabbi Neulander and by all the sages who guide us on our journey. This holy place, this M'kor Shalom, will be a different yet no less holy place. May we gain strength from each other, may we gain strength from our leadership as we join hands and move along our journey. Who knows where it may lead? We do know that as long as we are guided by our hearts, our heritage and our strength, it will be a meaningful journey. Together we will emerge stronger and continue to make a difference in our world. May we go forth together, in peace.

This was the most important sermon I had ever delivered up to that moment in my short career. My congregation was looking to me to lead them, help them, give them strength. I wanted desperately to get away, find solitude, to deal with my own sense of loss and tragedy. It was during February and March of 1995 that the image of the "burning bush" seemed so powerful to me. I was in the midst of personal flames. I wanted, as did Moses, to run. Yet, there were more powerful flames around me and there was a "calling," a need to respond.

Feeling almost like an unqualified impostor, I began what I anticipated might be the most important role I would ever serve as a rabbi. The bush was burning. But it did not have to consume us. In the midst of the flames was the opportunity for real healing and the emergence of personal and communal strength.

CHAPTER 4

# The Seventh Commandment

The next few months were intensely difficult for all of us. I often sat alone in the sanctuary during the week, pondering what had happened and how we got here. Above the Holy Ark (the large wooden structure which houses the Torah scrolls) were written the first two words of each of the Ten Commandments. I looked at them closely one day and was struck by how many had been violated in this terrible tragedy.

We had experienced murder. All of us watched murder mysteries on TV and shared a fascination with famous cases. But none of us had ever been so personally and profoundly affected by the vicious taking of a human life. Some of our innocence had been stolen. I was angry that my kids, then ages five and two, had to deal at such a tender age with the murder of their beloved "Aunt Carol." They were having nightmares about her murder, and this was a case where I couldn't blame television or video games for their exposure to violence.

The first two commandments affirm the place of God in our lives, and for many, this was truly a crisis of faith—a test of their faith in their God. Some answered by abandoning their faith. From my perspective as a spiritual leader, this just added to the tragedy's toll. Many of our congregants had actually placed their faith not in God, but in God's messenger, the rabbi. When the rabbi fell from grace, God and their Jewish identity were also called into question. I spent many hours counseling these people, trying to return them to their spiritual path.

The commandment at the root of the crisis of faith for so many was the seventh. *"Lo Tinaf"* in the Hebrew translates usually into *You shall not commit adultery.* Of all the Ten Commandments, the seventh seems to be the most problematic in our society. Governments have been toppled, families have been destroyed, and houses of worship have been decimated by acts of sexual impropriety.

In our case, one man's infidelities had affected a congregation of 4,000 individuals. If the most sacred relationship, that of husband and wife, had been betrayed by their spiritual leader, how could they believe *their* relationship with their rabbi had had any meaning for him? People were pouring into my office or calling my wife, trying to deal with troubling questions and complex emotions.

A complexity I faced—one that made much of my counseling ineffective—was that there had been no public acknowledgment of the affairs. The newspapers had intimated that there were "other women" involved. The rabbi himself spoke of ". . . behavior of which I am not proud . . ." in his letter of resignation. Yet none of the details I carried around in private had been made public, and I was bound by my own stricture against hurtful talk.

I could let others talk and I would listen intently. I had to counsel them that they really didn't know whether the rabbi was unfaithful or not. As I said this, I knew how ineffective I was being. Everyone knew what no one could say with certainty.

I urged people to hang on to the personally significant moments they had shared with the rabbi. I told them they had no reason to believe anything he had said or done for them was less than genuine. The words often fell on deaf ears. I was in a quandary. Do I reveal facts I know to someone who is struggling, if those facts will help them through their own turmoil? Do I share the truth to help others deal with a crisis of faith? Do I break the confidence I swore to the rabbi in order to help others in their healing process? The answer kept coming up "no." No matter how desperately I wanted to help, I couldn't share this knowledge. So it was *alleged* adultery until the newspapers, in their usual voyeuristic style, would help provide a strange form of resolution by revealing the truth.

That moment of truth came in the third week of August, 1995. For the first time since Carol's murder, my family and I had left Cherry Hill for a working vacation. We headed, as we did each summer, to our regional Reform Jewish camp for some badly needed rejuvenation. This was our spiritual home away from home. There we were safe from media phone calls and overwhelming hours of counseling, free to be with friends and family in a utopian environment.

The first week of camp was my first opportunity to begin processing the enormity of the task I faced. I was still, technically, the associate rabbi. Although I was the acting senior rabbi, there had been no commitment on either side to formalize that position. According to the rules of rabbinic placement, I was six years shy of being technically qualified for the job I was in fact performing. For the first time, I sought rabbinic counsel as to what *I* should do.

The answer was clear from every source I consulted. "Get out, Gary." "You can't succeed in this situation—no one can succeed in this situation." The message I got was that for the sake of my sanity and my career, I should leave. "The congregation will be OK," I was told. "Congregations can deal with tragedy and survive." Yet I felt deep in my heart that to leave would be to abandon this community. There was a real "burning bush" in our midst. I could watch the flames from a distance and move on with my life; or I could look within the flames and help a community re-establish a relationship with God. We had only begun to deal with the enormity of this tragedy and I knew more was on the horizon.

I could not leave. But I was not ready to commit to staying.

As I pondered my future and that of the congregation I began to relax for the first time in nine months. The relaxation was short-lived. The camp director came by our house late at night to warn me of what was happening on the news. I rushed up to his house to watch the TV. A very prominent woman in Philadelphia had gone public about a long-term affair with the rabbi—a relationship that was in progress at the time of the murder. The adultery was no longer *alleged*. Violation of the seventh commandment had reared its ugly head for real.

The phones at the camp began ringing off the hook. Somehow, the Philadelphia media had found out where I was. What was most disturbing was the array of techniques they used to try to get to me. The most blatant and offensive phone call came from, of all places, the Jewish press of Philadelphia. The reporter never stated that she was a reporter, and gave only her name when telling the office it was urgent they find me. It was clear I needed to leave immediately and return to Cherry Hill.

As if this news were not devastating enough, leaks from the prosecutor's office to the media confirmed what I had known since weeks after the murder: the rabbi was officially a suspect. By placing the adultery issue in the public domain, the media had in some ways freed my hand for rabbinic counseling on that issue. But suspicion of the rabbi's involvement in the murder itself was a far more difficult situation to handle.

I arrived home to an all-too-familiar scene. The news vans from every major network were in our synagogue parking lot. Reporters tried to interview members of the congregation on their way into the sanctuary. Photographers tried to force their way into the building. Once again, my office became a war room instead of a devotional room—planning strategy, writing press statements and electing a spokesperson. Our congregants were looking for a response. Once again, we affirmed that we would not engage in rumors and innuendo. The rabbi was no longer an employee of the synagogue. The events were tragic for all. We hoped and prayed there would be closure for Carol's family.

The media barrage opened the floodgates of emotions for members of the community. "Did you know all this?" I was frequently asked. "Did the leadership of the synagogue know all the details of the adultery and not tell us?" Some were hostile. Others suffered shame and embarrassment. Many had actually walked away from the synagogue because they believed we had done a great disservice to the rabbi by accepting his resignation. They had not believed the rumors of adultery, and we had not confirmed them. Now they were doubly devastated: betrayed by the man they loved, and separated from the community they so desperately needed. Much of my counseling was "door to door," trying to reach out to those who had left, assuring them that we welcomed them back, that they could and should come back. Few did.

*Betrayal:* perhaps the single strongest emotion felt after the media revelation of the adultery. To many, this rabbi had been the embodiment of Judaism itself. To be betrayed by him was to be betrayed by our religion. Worse, some felt *God* had betrayed them. This rabbi was a truly charismatic leader. He could inspire, anger and draw people close to him like few others. But charismatic leaders can be dangerous because they often inspire their followers' faith to focus on them, not God. And sometimes charismatic leaders act as if the ethics and morals they preach do not apply to them.

A letter from a prior student of mine provided the most powerful statement of that sense of betrayal. For her, the rabbi had *been* Judaism. The most meaningful moments of her life had been spent with him. He was there when she was called to the Torah as a bat mitzvah. He was there to help bury her loved ones. Now she felt deep betrayal and confusing emotions. There was no reason to stay committed to her faith, she wrote; her faith had been shattered.

As I answered her letter, I realized we were approaching the Jewish High Holy Days. The leaks from the prosecutor's office to the media meant I would have to find a way to make our High Holy Day celebration meaningful while dealing with these issues. The former student's letter became the basis for the message of one of my Rosh Hashanah sermons, the new "most important sermon" I had ever written:

> Another summer has come to an end, another summer of swimming, golf and camp. Like many of you, I put my boys on their respective buses and watched them journey toward their fun-packed days: Ari to the JCC camps at Medford, to romp in the woods, learn how to swim, catch worms, grow as a Jew and sing inappropriate songs on the bus. Daniel to kindercamp where he learned two camp songs he still hasn't stopped singing.
>
> There is sheer brilliance in the JCC's naming each of its three camp units after tree parts: roots, trunk and branches. This is a perfect metaphor for our kids growing up, for our synagogue, for Judaism itself. The metaphor of the tree is not foreign to us. At the dedication of this building five years ago, many of us wore our synagogue T-shirts which pictured a tree and the quote, "My roots are planted at M'kor Shalom."
>
> The tree is an important symbol for us. When we wish to honor or memorialize loved ones or to commemorate a key life moment, we plant trees in Israel or buy leaves to place on our tree of life. Many of us can walk over to that tree and see the history of our family unfold.
>
> We just put Torah back into the ark. As we did so, we sang *Torah is a tree of life to those who hold it fast.* The metaphor of the tree is strong for us and we will explore it on this day of focus on our souls and beings.

The foundation of the tree is the roots. What are *our* roots? What is the source of our strength, the foundation of our faith? Our T-shirts say that our roots are planted at M'kor Shalom. While our roots may have been planted here, the synagogue alone cannot be the root of our Judaism. There is great danger in viewing one place—or riskier yet, one individual—as the embodiment or the foundation of Judaism. Too often, the institution or the individual may fail in the eyes of the believer, leaving Judaism to be seen as worthless or useless.

I recently received a letter from a college student who is struggling with her faith. She is struggling because she now realizes that her faith had been put in one individual, and when that individual failed in her eyes, Judaism failed. She writes, "I am so confused about Judaism and being Jewish. There is so much about it that I love and I think is so beautiful, but at the same time I think it's changed." She then went on to describe the disappointment, the betrayal, the hurt she was feeling toward a significant role model in her life. ". . . he *was* Judaism to me, he was my connection to God. I see myself drifting away from the Jewish religion. I fought myself to stop believing in everything I believed in my whole life. I really don't see how I could ever follow another human being again. I've always loved being Jewish. I just don't believe in organized religion anymore."

When I first read this letter, my heart stopped. I cried. I thought, "How sad, how tragic!" After several readings, I realized how brave this young lady was and how well she was in touch with her emotions. I realized she was not alone. Too many people in this world worship individuals as the roots of their faith. So I responded, "First of all, I want to thank you for writing. I can only imagine how difficult it was to write that letter, and I am glad you chose to share your thoughts and your pain with me. What you can take from this experience is that no one *person* is Judaism. Judaism is a way of life. Judaism is the Torah, the holidays, the times shared with your family during the holidays. Judaism is the compilation of the lessons and values that your family, your heritage and your rabbis have tried to teach you. We follow ideals, philosophies and values, not individuals."

What then is the root of Judaism? The root of Judaism is our belief and faith in God. God is the foundation. God is perfection, for which we strive yet never reach. The laws, the values and the beauty of Judaism are rooted in the drama of the relationship between ourselves and God.

At times our faith is shaken—often by tragedy. For some, faith is difficult because of personal losses or unanswered questions. Judaism has always encouraged us to question and challenge God. There are always unanswered questions. Our Shabbat prayer book contains this beautiful passage:

> *Praise me, says God, and I will know that you love me. Curse me, says God, and I will know that you love me. Praise me or curse me, and I will know that you love me. Sing out my graces, says God. Raise your fist against me and revile, says God. Sing out graces or revile, reviling is also a kind of praise, says God. But if*

> *you sit fenced off in your apathy, says God, if you look at the stars and yawn, if you see suffering and don't cry out, if you don't praise and you don't revile, if you do nothing, then I created you in vain, says God.*

God is our *shoresh*, the root of our being.

Climbing up from the roots we find the strength and stability of the tree: the trunk. If God is the root of our Jewish identity, then the body of Judaism—its strength and perseverance—is Torah. It is Torah that has guided and inspired us through the ages. Too often we forget that the trunk that supports us is Torah. It is a tree of life to those who hold fast to it, and its supporters are happy. To be happy with Torah is to live by its guidance, to live by its code.

Last night I spoke about one panel of our windows. Now let me call your attention to another. Running through the bottom half of the stained glass windows is a scroll. This scroll is probably blue or magenta, depending on your seat. If we were to come into this sanctuary at night, the scroll would be almost gold. If you are in the nosebleed section, you can't see the scroll so you will have to trust me.

I had the opportunity to be a part of the selection of glass for this particular section of the windows. When I began to describe the concept of Torah to the artist I spoke of a document that is ever-changing. I told him that Torah is never the same to any two people, and that at different stages in our lives we view its words and messages in a new light. Torah is timeless.

Sadly, I have heard time and time again this year that Torah has lost its value. So many have come to me, as did the young lady who wrote the letter, and said they think the message is no longer valid. Young and not so young people look around their world and see that the words of Torah, the values of Torah, are not being lived out. They see poverty, war and famine rampant in our world. They see their heroes fall. They see those they assume will live their life by the values in Torah disappoint and disillusion them. Then they draw the conclusion that if the messengers of Torah are no longer valid, the message must no longer be valid.

This is a classic case of misdirected anger. Yet people struggle to find meaning when they see their world and the system of values they have been taught since they were young come crashing down. We need to remind them and ourselves that Torah is timeless. Just because the messengers of Torah are imperfect and perhaps disappointing does not mean that the message is bad.

Our Shabbat prayer book teaches us,

> *Let us affirm our faith in Torah, our people's legacy of learning and faith. There are no words more challenging than "You shall be holy." No command more basic than "You shall love." There is no insight so fundamental as "In the beginning, God . . ." No words so life-enhancing as "You shall rest." No cry is more compelling than "Let my people go." No consolation more comforting than "I am with you in your distress." There is no vision more hopeful than "They shall beat their swords into plowshares," and no summons more*

*demanding than "Justice, justice shall you pursue!" These words have outlived monuments and empires. We want them to live through us until the end of time.*

*We owe it to our ancestors to keep Torah alive. They struggled and suffered to preserve our way of life; they knew this to be their most precious gift to us. We owe it to our children to keep Torah alive; for why should they be spiritual paupers when the riches of this heritage can be theirs? We owe it to the world to keep Torah alive; this is a message the world needs to hear. We owe it to God to continue as a people, to share God's dream, to bear witness to God's sovereignty and to live the words of Torah.*

We owe it to ourselves to keep Torah alive. It is our tree of life and strength.

The tree's color, beauty and depth come from the students of Torah, our children. They are the leaves and branches of the present and the seeds of the future. Parents must plant the seeds and nurture them until they can flourish on their own. The seeds of Jewish life and learning must be planted in a positive, strong Jewish environment. Children must then use those lessons taught by their parents to forge their own way in the world.

Once the seeds are planted, our job as parents is not complete. The seeds need nourishment, cultivation, support and love. This is where parents and synagogue can work together. One of the most important ways this goal can be achieved is by providing Jewish options for our kids as they get older.

In a world where it is a real and viable choice to opt out of a Jewish way of life, our children need vehicles, role models and opportunities for positive, meaningful and effective Jewish expression. Major studies have been done recently trying to determine, "What keeps our kids Jewish? What keeps the branches connected to the tree?" Continued Jewish education through bar/bat mitzvah and beyond, and experiencing Judaism in the home are important. But perhaps more than any other factor, the studies tell us that what most solidifies the Jewishness of our future is an experience in Israel.

Walking in the footsteps of Abraham and Sarah, Isaac and Rebekah, Moses, Deborah and all those who shaped our Jewish past helps solidify our Jewish future. Now, finally, we have that opportunity. This year, during winter break, I will accompany this year's and last year's confirmation classes on a sacred pilgrimage to the Holy Land. It is my hope that each and every one eligible for this once-in-a-lifetime opportunity will join me as we plant the seeds together for our collective Jewish future. Israel will help our branches, leaves and flowers to blossom. For only a blossom can produce the seeds of the future.

These are the words of one of my favorite authors, Robert Fulghum, from his book *Uh Oh:*

> *There is a tree. At the downhill edge of a long, narrow field in the western foothills of the La Sal Mountains—southeastern Utah. A particular tree. A juniper. Large for its species—maybe 20 feet tall and 2 feet in diameter. For perhaps 300 years this tree has stood*

> *its ground. Flourishing in good seasons, and holding on in bad times. "Beautiful" is not a word that comes to mind when one first sees it. No naturalist would photograph it as exemplary of its kind. Twisted by wind, split and scarred by lightning, scarred by brushfire, chewed on by insects, and pecked by birds. Human beings have stripped long strings of bark from its trunk, stapled barbed wire to it in using it as a corner post for a fence line, and nailed signs on it. No matter what, in drought, flood, heat and cold it has continued. There is rot and death in it near the ground. But at the greening tips of its upper branches and in its berrylike seed cones, there is the outreach of life.*

I respect this old juniper tree. For its age, yes. And for its steadfastness in taking whatever is thrown at it. That it has been useful in a practical way beyond itself counts for much, as well. Most of all, I admire its capacity for self-healing beyond all accidents and assaults. There is a will in it toward continuing to be, come what may.

The tree in this story is us, collectively and individually. The tree is Judaism. The tree is M'kor Shalom. Like this tree, we have engaged in self-healing. There is a will in us as well; a will to go back to our roots, and draw strength from God. There is a will to reconnect with that which has given our people stability over the years: our trunk, the wisdom of Torah. And there is a will to continue doing the work of ensuring our Jewish future by allowing our branches—our children—to connect with our Jewish past and grow as positive, confident Jews. M'kor Shalom is all this, and we will continue and thrive come what

> may. May we journey along that path together and draw strength from one another.

The reaction was overwhelming. Never have so many people requested a copy of one of my sermons. Parents wanted to send copies to their kids who couldn't or wouldn't come home from school that year.

But the reaction wasn't all positive. The rabbi had actually stepped back into the sanctuary for the holidays that year and brought his children. Two weeks before the holidays, I had shared with him that I needed to address his resignation and the related issues with the congregation. He said he was disappointed, but he understood. I pleaded with him to tell his children so they wouldn't be, to use a term he often used, "sandbagged" on the holiest day of the year. He chose not to tell them. And it irreparably harmed my relationship with each of them to this day.

I have often second-guessed that sermon. Each time I do, I am reminded that there were 2,000 people there who needed to hear the message that Judaism does not worship people. We worship God. They needed to hear that others felt the betrayal they were feeling. They needed to hear that this and every congregation is about more than its leader.

As I concluded that morning's sermon, what was so striking was the impact one man's violation of the seventh commandment had had on a community of almost 4,000 individuals. There was not a soul in our congregation who had not been affected in some way by the rabbi's adultery. We too rarely stop and imagine how our actions, our personal or moral lapses, can affect so many beyond our immediate circle.

Clergy, along with other community leaders, are invested with tremendous power and control. Yes, we are only human. But a heavy burden of responsibility comes with our ordination, a burden we can't avoid. The nature of our sacred offices makes it certain we will have a profound impact on countless lives; so we *must* be held to a higher standard.

CHAPTER 5

# "There are Stars"

I hung onto many images as a source of strength during those weeks and months, and I shared some with the congregation. Perhaps the image that gave me the greatest hope and motivation to move forward was from the Far East. Anyone who has ever attended a management seminar or listened to a motivational speaker has heard that the Chinese ideogram for "crisis" is actually a combination of the symbols for "danger" and "opportunity."

From the synagogue's perspective, this crisis certainly had the potential for plenty of danger. We ran the risk that our members would flee in large numbers to other synagogues which were free from scandal and intrigue. Initially, some members did leave. Some found the crisis a convenient time to cease their affiliation and blame organized religion for providing them with nothing but disappointment. There was fear that the synagogue might have to fold up its tent and shut its doors.

Some of our members found it difficult just to walk through the doors of the building. Each time they entered they were filled with memories of what had been. Perhaps they remembered Carol and all she meant to them.

Perhaps they remembered a significant moment in their lives which had been sanctified by the rabbi. Some questioned the sincerity of those moments, given their newfound information. I tried to assure each and every one that they should hang on to those memories and cherish them. I tried to explain that they had no reason to think the rabbi was anything but genuine and truly concerned for them at those times. But many felt pain too deeply to hear my words.

During those High Holy Days of 1995, my goal was to help our congregants begin to see the opportunity in the midst of the flames of crisis. We needed to provide people with concrete symbols and ideas they could grasp and use to pull themselves through the darkness, toward the light of hope. We had to move through this crisis by finding ways to grow, individually and communally. Opportunity was all around us.

One of the first opportunities for growth and healing came in the form of a project the synagogue had embarked on just prior to Carol's death. We had explored the possibility of illuminating our sanctuary with the beauty of stained glass windows. The rabbi and I had visited a local artist chosen for this very special project. We helped him design a meaningful, thematic series of windows.

The sanctuary in our building was both beautiful and stark. The abundance of wood gave a sense of warmth, yet the height of the ceiling gave the room a feeling of emptiness. Above the large wooden doors of the Holy Ark, which contained the sacred Torah scrolls, was an opening that had originally been designed for stained-glass windows. The windows for that opening gave us the opportunity to take a meaningful symbolic step toward healing.

It had been almost a year since Carol had been murdered. Somehow, the focus seemed to have shifted to the rabbi. Wasn't Carol the victim here? Didn't the violation of the seventh commandment further illustrate how tragic her life and death had been? As a congregation, we were wrestling with how best to remember Carol in the midst of the chaos around us.

The windows took on new meaning. They were a way to shine some light into the darkness that had befallen Carol, her family and the congregation. The windows spoke to us of the permanent light that Carol had radiated upon our lives. *M'kor Or* we called them—the Source of Light. For Carol had been a source of light, and her memory was a source of strength to us all. Here is the sermon I gave our faith community to bind the light of God that would shine through our windows with the light of God that shone through Carol.

> The time was 11:59 PM. The place, COMPUSA. The date, August 23. Yes, your rabbi is a certified (and possibly certifiable) computer geek. But I admit I was there, ready for the clock to turn to 12:00 AM on August 24. This was to be the most important moment in computer history and I was not about to miss it! This was the debut of Windows '95, the most over-hyped piece of software ever developed. Yes, I was the first on my block to put it on my system, curse at it, and convince myself that it was the greatest thing since the Talmud.
>
> For those of you who didn't join me at COMPUSA, let me tell you my impression of Windows '95. Windows '95 has a spiritual component! (No, I haven't absorbed too much harmful radiation from sitting in front of my screen.) There is one little feature that speaks of creation

and new beginnings, and is very fitting for Rosh Hashanah. In the lower left-hand corner is a button called, appropriately, the "Start" button. To begin any project or function one must go to this button. Every time you write, calculate, research or compose you must look at the button that simply says "Start." Thus, there is a new beginning, a new creation, every time one sits in front of the screen.

Windows '95 is not the only "windows" that evokes this sense of re-creation and new beginnings. Putting Windows '95 to shame in terms of creativity and beauty is Windows M'kor Shalom. On August 22, Windows M'kor Shalom made its debut. Behind me are the stained glass windows designed by Paul Friend. These windows are full of meaning and beauty, and I guarantee that their usefulness and spiritual worth will far outlast Bill Gates's newest venture. We will officially dedicate these magnificent windows in November; then I will teach about their meanings and subtleties.

Tonight I'd like to focus on the window in the top left corner. Depicted in that window is a representation of the sun. This window speaks to us of creation. We are reminded of God creating light. The beauty of this panel depicting the creation of light is that it never looks the same. The craftsmanship and design make the view, the colors, and the depth different from every seat in this sanctuary. The colors are different in the morning from those we see in the evening. Each time we look, we see something new. When we enter this sanctuary, now more than ever, we see a new light and are reminded of the creative potential within us all.

Since this is Rosh Hashanah, the birthday of the world, it is appropriate to speak of creation. Tradition teaches us that each Rosh Hashanah is not only an opportunity to celebrate the world that has been given to us by God, it is an opportunity for each of us to start again. Each year we start anew. We look ahead to this New Year with new thoughts and dreams. Each year we get another chance to invest our lives with new meaning, creativity and purpose. Each year our perspective—like our windows—changes. This past year, our perspective had to change in so many ways.

Light, hope, and the beauty of potential were absent at M'kor Shalom at times this past year. Some look back upon 5755 as a year of darkness, despair and gloom. Yes, this was a year unlike any we have experienced—a year of loss and tragedy. We were shaken to our core, overcome by grief, confused and conflicted. This Rosh Hashanah, this day of creation, some of us may regrettably be thinking of destruction rather than creation.

Tonight we feel again the loss of Carol Neulander. Earlier, as Debbi lit the festival candles, I could not help but remember that this was Carol's honor for 21 years. Somehow it seems strange and difficult for anyone else to take that honor. Yet we must go on. The candles must continue to glow. The light needs to shine. This is a painful time; but creation, re-creation and change are never easy.

It is easy to get weighed down by the pain, the loss, the anger and the confusion. Look again to the window behind me. We could look up to the symbol of creation and see the colors not as brilliant, but lifeless. That decision is up to us. Often during this past year, I stumbled under the weight of my own emotions. There were times I, too, was disillusioned and angry at the sudden changes and new demands placed upon me. I was confused and conflicted. I could not see the light shining through; I saw only darkness.

Sages teach us that darkness is simply the absence of light. If we allow the light to shine through, the darkness dissipates. It took me many months to get beyond the pain and the darkness. Without support and an occasional loving kick in the pants from Debbi, and the unconditional support of this synagogue's leadership, I'm not sure I would have made it.

I know many of you dreaded coming here tonight. "Would things be the same?" you might have thought. No, things will never be the same. By definition they must be different. Different, however does not mean darkness or the absence of light. Difference can mean potential—the promise of a new beginning, a new light.

Sara's birth this past April helped me put life back in its proper perspective. She emerged as a new, brilliant light, a gift from God, a reminder that life continues. As many of you know, she is named in part for Carol. She is a constant reminder of our friend, and an ever-present symbol that her memory burns on within our lives. Now, bringing a new baby into your lives may not be the answer for everyone, but maybe it's worth considering! We must all find meaning and light.

Light is very much present at M'kor Shalom. We must look for it, see it, experience it and cherish it. We must, as with Windows '95, click on our Start button and begin anew. We have the power and responsibility to create. It is incumbent on each and every member of this congregation to send forth the message that this synagogue is strong, vibrant and dynamic.

Since the creation of the first Sanctuary, the presence of light has indicated the presence of God. Fire—a powerful representation of God—was visible in the midst of the Sanctuary. We need only look above the ark to see the eternal light, the symbol that God is with us. We must look within the flames that surround our lives and find the presence of God there as well—as our prophet Moses did.

The flames that burn within our lives are the flames of our faith. The eternal flame that glows above the ark tells us God is near. The inscription on our eternal light means *the light of God is the soul of humanity.* This light compels us to see God in the midst of the fire; to not let darkness—the absence of light—rule our lives. These are the flames that compel us to fight injustice and hatred; the flames that teach us to clothe the needy and feed the hungry and house the homeless. These are the flames of Judaism. This is what kindles our spirit and gives us purpose. This is what we have been taught from this pulpit and what we in turn teach our children. That we can make a difference. That Judaism gives us a blueprint to change the world.

So we move forward. Each time we enter this sanctuary we will look up at these windows and be reminded of important things. These windows will not come crashing down, unlike the Windows on my laptop.

> These windows were installed in only two days but will last a lifetime. Windows '95 has taken weeks to get right and will be outdated by this time next year.
>
> These windows we call *M'kor Or*, the Source of Light, speak to us of creation and purpose. Each time we look at them we will see something new. Their light and warmth will grace each moment of significance that occurs in this sanctuary. Within these walls we experience the heights of joy and pride as we name our children and celebrate their bar/bat mitzvahs and their confirmation services. Within these walls we experience the depths of despair after we lose one we love and hear their name read aloud. Within these walls we have experienced tragedy and ecstasy. Within these walls, the drama that is Judaism has unfolded before us. This is our home. This is a safe place, a place we need to be part of. Here we will continue to create, innovate and experience the beauty of Judaism. Tonight, we must click on that "Start" button and move forward. Tonight, we must "Start" to begin anew. Tonight, we must "Start" to cease dwelling in the past and "Start" beginning to shape our future. May we move forward together from strength to strength.

This was not an easy sermon to get through; yet it was profoundly important for me and the congregation. They needed to see me in control. They needed to be led and guided and assured there would be hope in the darkness. Despite my reluctance, I needed to assume that role. No longer could I be the "kid," the junior rabbi. I needed to be their rabbi and guide them through the valley of the shadows. That night solidified in the minds of the synagogue leadership that we could go forward together.

We hired an interim rabbi to help us that year. The congregation wanted to make a statement, so they moved me into the big office and placed the interim rabbi in my office. He was a great help and a stabilizing presence. His role was to provide some stature and stability to the congregation. He was more than twice my age, which gave us a nice balance, and made him a valuable resource to many who wanted a "parental presence" to talk to. He helped guide the congregation to the decision to name me senior rabbi that October, effective the following July.

Perhaps his greatest gift to the congregation was the time he spent with the cantor and me. We were devoting countless hours trying to help members of the congregation heal; but who was there to help *us* heal? We needed someone we could go to who was objective and removed from the crisis. I needed a rabbi on site to guide me in the deeper issues the members of the congregation were facing. I also needed someone who had been around the block a few times to reassure me that I was being effective, and guide me in reaching down deep to fulfill my potential as a rabbi. Initially, I had scoffed at the idea of an interim rabbi with no connection to the congregation. As his year came to a close, I realized how much he had helped me deal with my pain and the enormous task of helping this congregation heal.

In November, 1995, we officially dedicated the stained glass windows in the sanctuary. Another spoke had been added to the wheel of healing. A piece of original music was commissioned from a world-famous Jewish composer in Cincinnati, Professor Bonia Shur, in memory of

Carol. It was entitled *Yesh Cochavim,* meaning "There are Stars." Here are the remarks I delivered at the dedication service after this chilling and inspiring song:

> This piece of music, which we all just experienced for the first time, touches our souls. It is about the people we have all lost. It is inspired by the communal loss of Carol Neulander. It gives strength and hope to the Neulander and Lidz families, and to us all.
>
> *There are stars whose radiance is visible on earth though they have long been extinct.* This stanza speaks about the power of memory. It is no accident that this piece debuts tonight, for tonight is the *Yartzeit*—the anniversary of Carol's death. We Jews have long understood the power of memory. We are commanded four times a year to remember those stars—those loved ones—whose memory, whose radiance is so visible in our daily lives. They shine that much brighter as we bring them to the forefront of our minds. Carol's radiance can be experienced in each and every corner of this building and—most importantly—in each and every one of us. She touched our lives. She shared our joys, she shared our sorrows, she was an inspiration to us all.
>
> *Yesh Cochavim* continues, *There are people whose brilliance continues to light the world though they are no longer among the living.* Carol's brilliance gives light to us all. She was a driving force in the building and forming of this synagogue. She was an ever-present part of the life of M'kor Shalom. She has been and continues to be remembered in so many ways. She shines on through the brilliance of the music we just heard and through the

brilliance of the light that streams from the windows above me.

*Yesh Cochavim* concludes with the verse: *These lights are particularly bright when the night is dark; they light the way for humankind.* The loss of Carol left us in darkness. Yet this piece reminds us that at those moments when we feel most alone in a world that seems without light, *there is light.* There is a particularly bright light. And that is the light of Carol's memory.

On this weekend of Thanksgiving we remember the light that is Carol Neulander, and we give thanks for the moments shared and the memories that continue to shine bright. On this weekend of Thanksgiving we give thanks to God for the gift that was Carol's life. On this weekend of Thanksgiving we give thanks for M'kor Shalom—this source of peace and strength and comfort. May we find the radiance that was Carol's life within the walls of this sanctuary. May we find the brilliance of Carol through the beauty of memory. And when the night is dark may we look up to the sky and see that *There are Stars.* The memory of those we loved shines forth. As we sanctify their memory and remember their lives, the stars will glow brighter and brighter. May the memory of Carol Neulander live on for a blessing; and we say, "Amen."

CHAPTER 6

# Reaching In, Reaching Out

Although we dealt with difficult issues during those High Holy Days of 1995, we began to see opportunities for healing and strength. Those who left the community were gone, but those who remained banded together. They knew this congregation had the strength to survive. We were not going to fold our tent. We were not going to give in to the hovering black cloud.

We began to move forward.

That winter, with the interim rabbi contributing to the day-to-day needs of the synagogue, I was able to spend more time with members of the congregation processing their emotions and helping them mend.

In the spring of 1996, I became the youngest senior rabbi of a large congregation in the country. I was 32 years old and, in one sense, in a position many rabbis would dream of as the culmination of their entire careers. But this was never what I anticipated or desired for myself—and particularly not as the result of such horrific events. My goal was to be rabbi to a community of about 300 families somewhere on Cape Cod—not 1,000 families in suburban Philadelphia. However, I had to believe that I had been put in this place at this time for a reason.

In July, we hired an assistant rabbi who quickly became a dear friend. He brought us youth, vitality, and—perhaps most importantly—no connection to the tragedy. He was there to help us create new programs, to be my partner in leading the congregation into the future. With our cantor, we presented the congregation with a leadership team bonded firmly to one another and committed to the overwhelming task at hand.

Something magical started that summer: our congregation began to grow again. New members with little or no connection to the previous rabbi emerged to catch some of the enthusiasm we were radiating. By no means were we safely through the valley of the shadow. In many ways that journey was just beginning. But we had a sense of purpose and a sense of community.

The top priority over the next couple of years would be to help our people over the issues that were still stumbling blocks to their healing. I spent a great deal of time in intense counseling with members of the congregation. Individuals who had been questioning the sincerity of acts performed by the rabbi felt a need to re-consecrate some of those moments. My initial approach was always to emphasize the presumption of his sincerity. But when that failed, creative rituals were needed.

One of the most difficult issues was religious conversion. Conversion to Judaism is an intense and lengthy process. One needs to demonstrate a desire to study and experience Judaism before he or she can even begin to make a formal decision to convert. The rabbi had sponsored many people for conversion during his years at the synagogue.

The difficulty came when the woman who had gone public about her relationship with the rabbi also revealed information about her conversion in the secular media. She, like many others, had been a student in my "Basic Judaism" class and was sponsored by the rabbi. Sponsorship usually entailed many meetings to discuss what had been studied in the classroom, and its relevance to life experienced outside the classroom. I had found this woman to be sincere and dedicated to her studies. I had never guessed that she was romantically involved with the rabbi. I remember her conversion vividly. We met at the local Orthodox synagogue to use their mikvah (the ritual bath used for spiritual and physical entrance into the Jewish community). She spoke with the witnesses present at her conversion. I was one of them. She told us how the rabbi had shown her the beauty of what it meant to be Jewish. We were all moved by her eloquent discourse, and welcomed her enthusiastically into the congregation.

She ended up bringing us pain. Soon after acknowledging her adulterous relationship with the rabbi, this woman relinquished her Jewish identity and publicly returned to her birth religion. Her conversion had been a farce. Those of us who participated were simply duped into believing she was committed to that which we hold so dear. The most sacred of ceremonies, the most potent of promises, had been defiled.

Another woman came to me with the desire to completely repeat her conversion process. She had begun to question the sincerity of the rabbi in the course of her entrance to Judaism. She was deeply committed to her new faith and wanted to erase any questions in her mind about the authenticity of her conversion. I took her, her husband and two other witnesses back to the mikvah. It was clear to me that she didn't need a re-conversion—even if that's what she felt this was. What she did need was a reaffirmation of her Jewish commitment: the opportunity to erase any doubt that her conversion was valid. It was a moving ceremony of renewal, a spiritual rebirth for all who were there.

More and more people came forward with feelings of profound betrayal. They were having difficulty finding the opportunity within the crisis. Their pain made me increasingly angry at the man I had once called my mentor.

Although the investigation was ongoing and the murder no closer to being solved, I did find time to put all that aside and focus on my personal life. The phone calls from the prosecutor's office became fewer, and the media frenzy had abated. My spirits, however, were not so easy to lift.

It had now been two years since the murder, and my life had changed in dramatic ways. I was no closer to my 300-family dream synagogue somewhere on Cape Cod. I was still in New Jersey with a large and growing congregation. I had a wonderful assistant rabbi, but the load was tough. We were a very small team managing what was really a large corporation with a multimillion-dollar budget.

My kids were growing up quickly. I found myself missing key events in their lives, and spending little time with my wife. She had left her job. Our family could not survive unless one of us was home and reliably available for our children.

I began to reflect a great deal on my daughter, Sara. Debbi had been pregnant with Sara at the time of Carol's death, and Sara was born less than two months after the rabbi resigned. She came into the life of our congregational family just when we needed something to give us hope and promise for the future.

Three hundred members of the congregation came to celebrate the ceremony where Sara received her Hebrew name, eight days after she was born. They needed her. In Jewish tradition, we name our children after those who have gone before us. Sara was named for Debbi's grandmother; her middle name, Rachel, was Carol's Hebrew name. We emphasized to the congregation at that ceremony that Sara would always carry Carol's name and memory.

But I was only on the periphery of Sara's life. My daughter was now in her second year and barely knew her father. I had negotiated a paternity leave in my contract but had never been able to take it, never been able to spend precious moments with her. To my dismay, I noticed feelings of resentment growing within me toward the demands of the synagogue—demands that separated me from my family. I began to feel trapped; not sure where I could or should go, and not feeling as though the synagogue were in a place where I could leave without pangs of abandonment guilt.

So the year passed.

For the High Holy Days of 1997, we created a new initiative called *M'kor Rachamim*—the Source of Compassion. The goal of the Source of Compassion was to reach out to every member of the congregation who was in any kind of need. We wanted to respond like a small community to such needs, and promote healing from within. It was the first time in three years that I felt we were starting something truly new and exciting. I offered two Rosh Hashanah sermons to officially launch *M'kor Rachamim*. In this first one, I wanted to start the congregation thinking about the societal challenges facing faith communities today, and the imperatives for being a successful synagogue of the future:

> There is a story told by Max Shulman about a woman who got in a fight with her rabbi. He writes:
>
>> *What happened was that Ma was cleaning a chicken one day and she found a little piece of something hard in the gizzard. According to the rules, if there's anything in the gizzard that's made out of metal, the chicken is not kosher. But you're not allowed to decide by yourself; you got to take the chicken to a rabbi.*
>>
>> *So off went Ma to Rabbi Greenberg and he took a look at the gizzard and said, "Too bad, missus. That's a cuff link."*
>>
>> *"What are you talking?" Ma said. "That's a piece of gravel."*
>>
>> *"With initials?" said the rabbi.*
>>
>> *So of course Ma did what everybody does in those cases: you eat the chicken and join a different shul.*

This story makes us laugh, to be sure. But it also contains a powerful message: the connection of many individuals to their synagogue is tenuous at best. Many leave their house of worship over little things. Their connection is not strong enough to overcome a crabby secretary (not that we would ever have such a thing); a rabbi who doesn't dress well (unheard of here); or a harmless remark taken the wrong way.

It used to be that one of the primary reasons for affiliation was a sense of ethnic belonging. So in one community we might have the Russian synagogue and in another the German synagogue. Now, as the overwhelming majority of American Jews are native born, there is no ethnic identification. Our ethnic selves are no longer the focus of our Jewish lives.

So why does a Jew join a synagogue in 1997? What should the synagogue of the 21st century be like? What will this synagogue of the future need to focus on to attract and retain its members? Professor Lawrence Hoffman authored an article for *Reform Judaism* in which he addressed these questions and tried to imagine the synagogue of the future. In his mind, one thing was very clear: the current model of the synagogue needs to drastically change if it is to survive in the next millennium. We need to strengthen the tenuous bond between congregant and congregation. The synagogue of the future needs to be a place that focuses on the individual as well as the community. The synagogue needs to be a place of inclusion and caring.

The synagogue must move away from the corporation-like structure of today. The current model of the synagogue has "management": the clergy and the staff working in conjunction with boards of trustees. Members of the synagogue are the "market." Clergy and staff are "product" or "product developers." The market buys the products, which are the life-cycle events, the religious education or the High Holy Day services and tickets. The synagogue is joined for a fee and then held liable for services rendered. Members behave like consumers and leave when the cost outweighs the services required or provided.

The synagogue of today is really no more than a limited-liability community. With this model, if the congregation's market share falls—meaning membership is down or attendance at events is poor—management is liable. The logical solution in some places is to get rid of the CEO—the rabbi. He or she is then terminated.

Dr. Hoffman sends a warning to today's synagogues when he states,

> *In these limited- liability communities, it is not uncommon for the rabbis to eventually complain about a "job" that ceases to be a calling. Their increased managerial duties within the corporation of the synagogue take them away from the study of Torah and the ability to minister effectively to their congregants. No one wins in the model that seems to pit the consumer against the producer or the board against the management. There is little that is spiritual in a system that encourages rapid burnout among professional and lay leaders alike.*

The synagogue of the future—the M'kor Shalom of the future—needs to be something very different. The M'kor

Shalom of the future needs to be a place where the primary focus is inclusion and caring.

And at which point do costs outweigh services? For too many, it's when the children finish religious school. Thus the synagogue is viewed as a place only for children or young families. Adults often feel excluded or superfluous. The synagogue of the future must address the needs of the grown-up. We must not consider just families with kids as our prime target market. We need to be a congregation of life-long participants and life-long learners. The study of Torah need not *stop* with bar/bat mitzvah training; it needs to *begin* there. Judaism has a great deal to offer adults. If we continue to primarily provide to parents vicariously through their kids, we will miss the boat completely. The M'kor Shalom of the future must be a place that stresses inclusion and caring, not just for kids but for all members of this synagogue.

We must, somehow, foster a greater connection to the synagogue. We need this to be a place that brings us in. When we drop off our kids there needs to be something for *us* to do as well.

We also need to reach out. No longer can we simply accept that some are "twice a year" Jews while others are "involved." If we do not see someone here during the year, then we are not reaching out to that person. In some congregations, the dues-paying member who has grown kids and makes no demands on the professional staff is viewed as the ideal member. This is so sad. Everyone should be involved.

So what do we do? What should the M'kor Shalom of the future look like, and how can we make it happen? As we near the next millennium, M'kor Shalom needs to shift its focus. We can move away from the corporate model and set the right tone for the future. We have always been "cutting edge." Let's move forward. Let's become the synagogue of caring and inclusion.

We need to revitalize prayer in the life our congregants. We need to help facilitate the ritualization of key moments in people's lives. Prayer needs to be engaging. Prayer also needs to be participatory. While we encourage participation, we can do more. So many view Friday evening as the only time to come to synagogue and participate in services. Shabbat morning and afternoon seem to have been lost, given over to the bar/bat mitzvah. We have created a mood of exclusion that is felt by many on, of all days, Shabbat.

This year we are planning something new to bring people back to their synagogue on Shabbat. Each of our committees has recently adopted a Shabbat. They have taken one Shabbat, and designated it as a time when the committee members and their families will attend and participate in the service by accepting honors. This will bring another piece of Shabbat into their lives. It is only a start.

Rabbi Daniel Silver writes:

> *I am a firm believer in public worship. I want to hold and read the liturgy of my people. The worship that I love is something finer and wiser than prayer. Prayer begins in need. Worship begins in reverence. Prayer is a measure of man's anxiety. Worship is the measure of man's commitment. Prayer begins in the overheated heart. Worship begins in the reflective soul. Prayer is*

> *half formed—a thing of the moment. Worship is sculptured—a thing of beauty. Prayer is an urgency. Worship is a discipline. We pray when life is too much for us. We worship, the better to live.*

We need more opportunities for meaningful worship in our lives. Reclaiming Shabbat can be one of those opportunities.

Last year you left the High Holy Days with a piece of paper to put on your refrigerators: a page of prayers to recite on a daily basis. It is my hope that you have integrated this into your daily routine. We must recognize on a daily basis the role God plays in our lives. We need to foster spirituality as one of our primary goals.

"Spirituality" has become a new buzzword. It is a new word because it seems to be a new and ever-present need in our lives. It used to be that 20-year-olds knew what their future would be. There was a normative path on which they would travel. In today's world, 30- and 40-year-olds still struggle with what they want to be when they grow up. There is more uncertainty about the future. For both genders, but primarily for women, there is the ever-present conflict of work and home. We are torn between the various worlds in which we live. We're not happy with many of the decisions we've made, but feel there is simply no choice. So we try to make the best of the struggles, tensions, busy schedules and familial demands. Spirituality, a relationship with our community and our God, can help us.

As Dr. Hoffman teaches us, a generation of baby boomers has become a generation of seekers, while their grandparents have become the first generation of grandparents free to move into retirement communities. However, they have had to substitute strangers for neighbors and phone calls for the hugs of grandchildren. The call for spirituality is a response to this new age of freedom. As Dr. Hoffman continues, "It is the conviction that where mandated communities called 'families' have collapsed, communities of choice called 'synagogues' can be centers of vision, hope, insight and care." These communities foster intellectual, emotional and spiritual fulfillment.

The synagogue of the future—the caring and inclusive synagogue—must address the needs of the lifelong learner. My vision of the M'kor Shalom of the future is a place where the study of Torah and Judaism is at the core of who we are and what we do. Lifelong study for all age groups needs to be addressed in greater detail than ever before. No longer can the norm be that parents drop off their kids in the parking lot and never set foot in the building. No longer can the message we send our kids be, "You need to learn about your heritage. I learned about it when I was a kid." The message must be, "Follow my example; see that I, too, study my Jewish past. Learn from what I do and the example I set that this place is a place where I also go to school—and will for the rest of my life."

Leonard Fein points out, "The purpose of Jewish education is to increase Jewish competence. Such competence cannot be defined exclusively in terms of mastery of texts or of rituals. Judaism is not only our birthright; it is our conviction, and competence at the expression of that conviction is therefore an essential aim of Jewish education." Competence is not reserved for the young. Education of young and old alike is one of the keys to Jewish survival as well as Jewish spiritual fulfillment.

In addition to a focus on strengthening our spirituality, the M'kor Shalom of the future must be a place where *righteousness* is a foundation value. Righteousness, social action and social justice cannot be merely the job of one committee. Doing our part to repair this fractured world we live in needs to be the focus of each and every individual in this synagogue. Reform Judaism has always maintained that our mandate is to continue the work of the prophets, the work of lighting a spark in the hearts of humanity; a spark that compels us to treat one another with dignity and respect; a spark that moves us to better our world.

There is a story of a man who went to his physician to complain about his heart.

> *The physician told him to stretch out his hand so that he might feel his pulse.*
>
> *"But doctor" said the patient, "It is my heart that I am complaining about."*
>
> *"I know," said the physician, "but from your hand and its pulse I can tell you about your heart."*

The soundness of our hearts can be judged from the work of our hands. When the pulse of righteousness doesn't beat strongly in the life of the Jew, it indicates a weakening of our total Jewish self.

Leonard Fein states, "A living Judaism—or, as Mordecai Kaplan called it, 'an evolving religious civilization'—doesn't ask, 'How shall we relate the doctrines of our faith or, for that matter, the story of our people to the pursuit of social justice?'" Such a living Judaism *is*, among other things, a pursuit of social justice. Even if we ourselves can't solve the American crisis, we can ease the pain of real people through our efforts, offering them a touch of dignity where they now have none. As Pirke Avot teaches us, "It is not for us to finish the work—but neither can we desist from it."

Rabbi Ya'akov Rosenberg tells us this story:

> *There once was a rich man who was on his deathbed. He gathered his children around him and said to them, "My children, I want you to sell everything I have. I want to liquidate all my assets and turn them into cash so I can take them with me when I go."*
>
> *The children were upset, but he insisted. He said, "I know they say you can't take it with you, but I don't believe that."*
>
> *So they bury him together with all his cash. He gets to the world to come and meets the angel Gabriel, and shows him all the money he has brought with him. And Gabriel says to him, "You don't understand. Here, it is not cash that is legal tender. Here, the only thing that counts is receipts."*

This story expresses an important truth. In the end, what really counts is not how much we have but what we have done with it, how many we have helped and how much we have shared. In the end, our only permanent possession is that which we have given away. Giving of ourselves—our money, our time, our love—helps to make us whole.

Lastly, the synagogue of the future also needs to be a place of healing and wholeness. We talk of this synagogue as an extension of our families; as a large family unit. Yet many feel alienated here, isolated and lonely. In an age of dissipation of the family, the synagogue needs, more than ever, to be that place that makes us feel safe, that makes us feel whole. As Dr. Hoffman explains, ". . . People will come to share their lives and their stories; to celebrate success and lament loss; to know, in sum, their connectedness to others; to glimpse, thereby, the reality of God and the profundity of spiritual renewal." When people feel their spirit is not whole, that it's broken in some way, the synagogue must be a place where the Jewish value of *wholeness* is felt.

My prayer this day is that we become a place that focuses on caring and inclusion, on spirituality and lifelong learning, on health and wholeness, on righteous acts. These are the foundational values of a strong M'kor Shalom, a synagogue which has meaningful bonds between the congregation and the community.

Throughout these holy days you will be hearing this theme. Each time your rabbis speak we will share with you our vision of where M'kor Shalom can go *now* to bring us into the future. Tomorrow morning we will unveil *M'kor Rachamim*, the Source of Compassion, our answer to this call.

In this second sermon from our 1997 High Holy Days, I focused on the spiritual connection and common humanity that represented the foundation of our new initiative:

> At this solemn time, on this sacred day, I am reminded of the famous one-line response given to Dustin Hoffman in *The Graduate.* Hoffman, the graduate, is sitting by the pool realizing that he has no idea what to make of his life or what his future will be. An older man, observing his angst, gives him advice: "Plastics; the future is plastics." Until I had kids, I never realized how prophetic that line would be.
>
> The reality is that my house is filled with plastic. Little Tykes, Fisher Price, Mattel, etc. You name it, if it's made of plastic it resides in my basement.
>
> Parenthood, as I have come to understand and appreciate it, is about the assembly of things made of plastic. Every fad has made its way to our home. This year's plastic "gotta have it" toy was perhaps the most interesting and the most disturbing to date.
>
> Tamagotchi, Nano Kitty, Nano Puppy: whatever kind your kid has, they are all the same. For those of you who managed to escape this latest fad, let me explain. These little plastic devices are about the size of a box of raisins and reside on a key chain. They are billed as "virtual pets." They are small computer-generated pets that "hatch" and are in need of your love and care. The kids have to feed them, play with them, give them medicine when they get sick, clean up after them and maintain their general level of happiness.

These lovable little plastic computerized pets beep every hour in search of attention. The defenders of these toys say they teach responsibility. If the kids don't care for them well enough, they either "die" or pack their bags and go away. So frantic kids entrust them during the daylight hours to their parents, who bring them to work, listen for the beeps and try their best not to kill their kids' pets. Virtual pets are now banned from most schools, activities, and even summer camps because of the noise and the stress they put on the kids. What a phenomenon! People pay $15 or $20 to become stressed out over the care of a plastic virtual pet!

Our kids agonize over the "lives" of these toys. Many are 100 percent devoted to their care. How many of these kids, though, devote as much time or energy to actual, real people in need? What of their parents? Just imagine what $20 could purchase for care of the real world. We are willing to pay to care for *something that is not real!* What does this say about our society? Perhaps if we put the lessons of the Tamagotchi into practice in our lives, this little piece of $20 plastic would have some merit.

Last night I introduced what may be the most important initiative this congregation has embarked upon in many years: *M'kor Rachamim,* the Source of Compassion. This is more than a new committee; it is about changing the priorities of our synagogue.

The Source of Compassion is our version of what is referred to throughout the Reform movement as "The Caring Community." Caring communities foster a sense of person-to-person involvement, as well as supporting one another within the framework of Jewish tradition. A caring community compels us to open our hearts to those in need of support within our synagogue family.

There is a story about a distinguished doctor who was called to a patient who had passed out and couldn't be revived.

> *The doctor examined the man and found all his limbs cold. He felt the patient's head—no warmth of life. He felt the patient's hands, which were cold. His feet were icy.*
>
> *The family saw that the doctor found no warmth and began to weep. The doctor said, "Don't despair yet, because I have not yet felt his heart." And so it was when he felt his heart, he found it warm and pulsating. The doctor said to the family with joy, "Dear children! There is hope that your father will recuperate for there is still a thread of life in his heart. Get warm water to warm him and he will revive. But don't delay with the warm water; it is vital."*

At this season we are taught that God is like this doctor. God feels our head; it is cold due to false thoughts. Our lips are cold because we use them for gossip. Our hands are cold because we use them for that which is prohibited. Our feet are cold because we use them to go where they should not go. But we should not despair. When God feels our heart it will be warm. There is hope. A community of caring gives us hope. The Source of Compassion will give us the warmth we need to revive our body's soul.

This year, it is our goal to reach out and extend a caring hand and a warm heart in three distinct areas:

▲ We will better fulfill our duty to visit the sick, infirm and shut-in.

▲ By empowering our lay community, we will improve our comforting of the bereaved.

▲ We will provide regular opportunities for practicing spiritual healing to achieve wholeness.

Traditional Morning Prayer teaches us there are . . . *obligations without measure, whose reward, too, is without measure.* One of those obligations is visiting the sick. In our community, this can involve a visit to a hospital, an elder care facility, a rehab center or someone's home. While the rabbis and cantor will always visit those who are infirm, it is my desire to expand spiritual support beyond the clergy's one or two visits to include visits by lay members of our community trained in pastoral care.

For six weeks in the spring, my wife will train a group of lay volunteers to become visitors to those in need. Debbi will teach the Jewish way of visiting the sick, infirm, elderly and shut-in. Her program, which has been tried and tested by the Philadelphia Board of Rabbis and the Hospital of the University of Pennsylvania, will open our eyes to the needs of those around us, and empower us to help.

Those who are not well need recognition by and connection to the community at large. We read from an anonymous source:

> *I am not the stroke in bed two, or the hip replacement in room four, or the bandage that needs changing in seven. I AM ME. I used to have responsibilities like you.*

> *There were people dependent on me. I had a wife, I raised seven children, I have made decisions. My body was young and strong. I ran, I flew, I made love, I ran with the wind, skimmed the lake in a sailboat. I have lain alone on smooth grass. I have kissed hurts away from skinned knees, and felt a baby's face nuzzling into my neck. I remember the fragrance of baby powder. I have been brave. I have won honors. I have failed in some things, but please see ME. You will be old someday just like ME. Then you will understand how I want you to know ME. But then it will be too late.*

We each have within us the power to make a difference in this man's life. We each have within us the power to make a difference in the lives of so many within our synagogue. Imagine if this man received a visit from someone within his synagogue—someone who went to see him because they cared and felt a family member was in need. His eyes light up as he hears, "I am part of your family. I am part of M'kor Shalom. Know that I am here, know that I see you and that I care." This is the spirit of the Source of Compassion.

Albert Einstein wrote,

> *Strange is our situation here upon the earth. Each of us comes for a short visit, not knowing why, yet sometimes seeming to devise a purpose. From the standpoint of daily life, however, there is one thing we know. That man is here for the sake of other men. . . . Above all, for those upon whose smile and well-being our own happiness depends, and also for the countless*

> *unknown souls with whose fate we are connected by a bond of sympathy.*
>
> *Many times a day I realize how much my own outer and inner life is built upon the labors of my fellow men, both living and dead, and how earnestly I must exert myself in order to give in return as much as I have received.*

Another area where our new program will make a difference is in comforting the bereaved. Sadly, many of us in this room have experienced firsthand the loneliness and despair that come with the loss of a loved one. We have walked aimlessly through the process of grieving. We endured the seemingly endless wait for the funeral. We sat shiva in our homes, greeted by friends, yet feeling lost and alone. Perhaps one of the clergy called, stopped by or led the funeral service or shiva service in your home. Perhaps you traveled to another state and went through the rituals of mourning without the comfort of your community and friends. We expect our clergy to be there when we are in town. We need our clergy. Yet we also need the ongoing comfort of our extended M'kor Shalom family.

Two years ago, Debbi and I began to address this need by training 12 incredibly dedicated volunteers who wanted to help the bereaved in our community. We trained these individuals in the laws and rituals of death and mourning. They were then trained to lead a shiva minyan in your homes. These dedicated souls pick up where the clergy leave off and provide continuing care to those in need. They also represent something the clergy can never be: peers, fellow congregants who simply care and want to show it.

The Source of Compassion will further this endeavor. We will soon offer follow-up training for those committed souls who have been our "minyanairs" for the last two years. We have all seen and experienced so much in our capacity as shiva leaders! This will give us a chance to process, share and learn from the past two years' experiences. We will then offer another opportunity for individuals to become trained as shiva leaders. Since we first began this program, many who have had shiva services in their homes or have attended minyans with their friends have expressed a desire to help fulfill this wonderful service to others. For two evenings we will again educate and train a new group of leaders.

Reaching out, showing compassion, treating fellow congregants like family: this is what our program is all about. We need your help to make this new venture work. Please reach out and let us help you. Too often, we learn of a loss when it is too late to provide this kind of support. Worse, feelings are often hurt and individuals actually feel abandoned by their synagogues and rabbis at their time of greatest need. If we don't know, we can't help. Help us help you. There is a beautiful poem that illustrates this point.

*If I had known*
*what troubles you were bearing,*
*what griefs were in the silence of your face,*
*I would have been more gentle and more caring,*
*And tried to give you gladness for a space.*

*I would have brought more warmth into the place—*
*if I had known.*

*If I had known*
*what thoughts despairing drew you—*
*why do we never understand?*
*I would have lent a little friendship to you,*
*And slipped my hand within your lonely hand,*
*and made your stay more pleasant in the land,*
*if I had known.*

Please let us know so we can be there for you.

Our new program will also address the need we all have for wholeness of body and spirit. During the past year we have routinely added a prayer of healing into our liturgy. Many have found this to be incredibly powerful, but we can expand on fulfilling this need. Once a month we will have a brief yet powerful service to facilitate spiritual healing. Many in the medical community have told us that spiritual healing and wholeness often brings physical healing and wholeness. The spiritually whole caregiver or family member is far more capable of helping the patient. And whether it is spiritual, mental or physical wholeness we seek, we all need healing.

We are taught this lesson by Rabbi Sanford Ragins:

*For a few weeks early this summer, for the first time in my life, I had to walk around with a cane. I had injured my foot in some obscure way, and the cane was not just for effect. It helped me get around, but it also caused unexpected things to happen. People opened doors for me. They gave me seats on crowded buses and some even offered to carry my packages.*

*Then, one day when I was in Jerusalem, I rested on my cane, waiting for a small elevator at our hotel. When the door opened, I saw a man in a wheelchair, about my age, with his wife. They filled the space, and there was no room for me, so I waved them on. But just for a second, before the doors closed, his eyes and mine met and there was a brief flash of empathy, a connection between two wounded spirits.*

*We never saw each other again, and I have been able to abandon the cane. But the memory of that chance meeting lingers with me and suggests a brooding metaphor for what the holy day season is all about.*

*We are all wounded by life. We can all benefit from healing. Some of us show it outwardly more than others, but no one escapes bruising. To live is to be hurt, and—sometimes inadvertently, sometimes not—to hurt others, even those closest to us. The fantasy that somehow we can get through life pain-free is just that: a phantasm of the mind; a mirage.*

The Source of Compassion is what the synagogue of the future must be: a place of caring, community and inclusion. We must reach out and reach in. Each of us has the potential to effect real change in the lives of members of our synagogue. Each of us can make the most difficult situation somehow more bearable for a member of our extended family.

> No longer do we have to pay to care for a virtual pet made of plastic and semiconductors. No longer is "caring" reserved for a $20 purchase made for our kids. Instead of cleaning up virtual poop we can provide real and meaningful care to those around us. Help make this synagogue a Source of Compassion. Help make this synagogue a synagogue of the future.

*M'kor Rachamim* continues to this day to make a difference in the lives of members of the congregation. That year we began a process of continued healing from within. A large institution of 4,000 souls was made a little more intimate. Mutual caring brought us closer as an extended family. The pain was still there; the hurt and betrayal did not go away easily. But when we began to reach back inside the family, the ache was a little more bearable.

The Jewish value of *shlemut* means "wholeness." The process of healing and moving through the crisis was really striving for wholeness. There were so many breaks, so many cracks, so many fragmented souls. We were searching for wholeness in a fractured world. We had begun to experience the opportunities for growth within the flames; we had begun to put the sacred back in our lives.

Maintaining that sacredness was the challenge. We didn't know yet just how difficult the challenge would be.

CHAPTER 7

# Profaning the Sacred

One of the most beautiful services in the Jewish religion is the service of *Havdalah. Havdalah* marks the separation of the seventh day, the Sabbath, from the other six days of the week. During the *Havdalah* service we use the sweetness of the wine to remind us of the sweetness of the Sabbath day. We then use the fragrant smell of the spices, usually contained in an ornate spice box, to remind us of the fragrant beauty of the Sabbath. As we take in the aroma of the spices, the hope is that the fragrant beauty of Shabbat will remain with us during the upcoming week. Finally, the large, braided candle is blessed. The candle speaks of the intertwining of Sabbath day holiness with the ordinary existence of the other days of the week.

In Hebrew, the word for "ordinary" also means "profane." Essentially, this service marks the boundary between the "sacred" and what can often be "profane"—the rest of our week. We try to escape the hectic routine of our daily lives during the sanctity of the Sabbath. On the Sabbath we no longer worship the almighty dollar; we worship only the almighty God. The clatter of commerce, the pursuit of personal gain and fortune, are all pieces of the ordinary and (sometimes) the profane in our lives.

In the aftermath of Carol Neulander's murder and the rabbi's resignation, we spent a great deal of energy helping people reclaim the sacred in their lives; the tragedy had worked to profane them. The sanctity of the rabbi, of sacred moments shared with a revered religious leader, the sanctity of the building and the philosophy of the synagogue itself had been profaned in many eyes. Some felt the image of the funeral taking place in the sanctuary had somehow made that room profane to them.

I had some control over the rate at which our people re-accepted the sacredness of our rituals and our synagogue. But I had no control over the ability of the investigation and the accompanying media frenzy to swiftly and convincingly strip that sanctity right back off again. Too often, that which was sacred to us as Jews was made profane by the insensitivity and callousness of those directing the investigation and those reporting on it.

The situations I found myself in ranged from impressively irritating to maddeningly surreal. One evening I met the prosecutor (the first of three to serve on this case) in the back room of a local diner. I had told him earlier in the day how the information leaks had devastated the congregation. Knowing that most prosecutors have political ambitions, I reminded him that a huge segment of the community was losing faith in him due to the shoddy investigation. Much worse, they were losing their faith in God. He assured me that no more leaks would be tolerated, and that he would issue a letter of apology to our synagogue and the entire community.

Next day he made a very public visit to the synagogue, where our leadership strongly advised him to issue a statement of explanation and apology regarding the leaks. He issued the letter later in the day; but the damage had been done. The holiest days of the year—perhaps the most important Holy Days in the lives of our congregants—had been profaned by the information put out on the street about the rabbi's private life, and the suspicion of his involvement in the murder itself.

The investigation moved from prosecutor to prosecutor to prosecutor. Each one, seemingly concerned with his political career, would check in with me from time to time to "see how the synagogue was doing." I extracted promises from all three of them that I would be notified before anything major occurred. I was also promised that the investigators would call before they showed up on my doorstep, which was becoming an all-too-familiar event. I tried to convey that this was not a story about the synagogue, and that each time members of the congregation saw a news story about the investigation their wounds re-opened.

The investigation reached a new low in the fall of 1996. It profaned the most sacred object in the synagogue: the Torah itself. The Torah contains the hand-written text of the first five books of the Hebrew Bible, The Five Books of Moses. It is the Torah that we Jews turn to for guidance, history and inspiration.

A wealthy businessman and friend of the rabbi had donated funds for a new Torah scroll to the synagogue in the spring of 1994, in memory of this man's wife: a most generous act. The investigators began to call me daily and ask questions about this Torah. They wanted to know where it came from, how much it cost, how much it was worth, and who sold it. I traced its history in our congregation and gave them as much information as I could. But I didn't understand their interest in this particular scroll.

Then I received a phone call that began an odd and painful odyssey for this Torah. The investigators asked (making it sound more like a demand) if I could be available to examine the scroll one evening when no one else would be around. They also asked if I knew a Torah expert who could help answer their questions. I arranged a meeting late one Tuesday evening.

There we were—the most bizarre scene yet in this unfolding mystery. Surrounding the Torah scroll—which was now laid out on the reading table—were the cantor, the synagogue president, two detectives, the scribe, Debbi and me. In later months we would relive this scene and mentally cast it for the made-for-TV movie. It was that bizarre.

The scribe is the individual who either writes the entirety of the Torah scroll or serves as "broker" to help congregations acquire a sacred Torah. Scribes are usually very pious Orthodox Jews, dedicated to their craft and the upholding of the sanctity of the Torah. This particular scribe had a full beard and wore the traditional dark suit and black *kippah* head covering. Debbi had engaged him to help repair a Torah at our local Jewish camp. He was reputable, honest as could be, and totally unaware of why he was needed. So was I.

The detectives then placed a bombshell in our laps: they believed this Torah might have been stolen and bought on the black market. I learned that there was indeed quite a black—or "gray"—market for used Torah scrolls. Since a new scroll could cost upwards of $30,000, many congregations jumped at scrolls priced from $5,000 to $10,000. Apparently, some of these were stolen.

The detectives were quick to defame the character of the donor of this scroll and intimated that perhaps the rabbi had had a part in the swindling. We were shocked and horrified that such allegations would be made surrounding an item so sacred to us. So we watched the scribe do his work. He methodically went through the scroll.

First he looked for identification marks. Many congregations identify their Torah scrolls by making small pinpricks in the lower margin in a unique pattern. Then they register that pattern with a national registry. We stood and watched in utter disbelief as this sacred scroll, used just the week prior at a bar mitzvah, was called into question. Thankfully, no identification marks were discovered.

We were not yet in the clear, however. As the scribe went through the sacred scroll, he noticed that it appeared to be a conglomerate of several scrolls sewn together. He pointed out deficiencies in the lettering and inadequacies in the assembly of the various panels of Hebrew text. In short, this was not a valuable scroll and no reputable scribe would have ever sold such a scroll to a congregation.

I was near tears. Our sacred scroll had been defiled before our eyes. "We just used this scroll," I thought. "How could we ever use it again?" It had been rendered useless. What do we do now? Who was responsible for this horrible situation? Why was this a necessary part of the investigation?

What the investigators were trying to do was discredit the rabbi in the eyes of those around him, thereby isolating him. They knew that he and I had been dancing around our friendship. They knew of my history with him, and that many in the congregation still supported him.

The rabbi had been my mentor and friend. He was at my wedding, and one of the first to hold my son Daniel after he was born. I had shared joy in his family and he had shared joy in mine. He had also placed me in an untenable situation due to his personal conduct. I was furious with him for taking so much of my life away from me. I was angrier for the pain he had caused so many others by his selfishness. Yet I still loved him. I was not ready to convict him of the murder as so many around me were doing. I needed to hang on to the possibility that he was not capable of murder. (In fact, I still need to hang on to that possibility.) The night around the Torah brought all these emotions once again to the surface.

Psychologists would say I was "conflicted." They'd be right.

I learned later that more than anything, the officials' objective in desecrating the sacred that night was to turn the donor of the scroll against his longtime friend, the rabbi. They wanted damning testimony from this man to link the rabbi to the murder. If they could prove that the rabbi had swindled the man out of money and purchased an un-kosher, unfit Torah, then perhaps he would turn on his friend. It was a brilliant strategy—and it worked. The donor eventually gave the prosecutor's office the testimony they wanted as a result of that painful and bizarre night around the scroll.

For the police, it was successful tactics. For us, it was the utter profaning of something sacred—a matter of little consequence to them. The pieces were purely ours to pick up. For those of us around the Torah that night, it was a sickening experience. The investigation had crossed the line of acceptable ethics. The desecration of the Torah, and how to handle this in our community, became a new consuming task.

We now had another dilemma on our hands. Those of us who knew about this scroll were once again privy to details of the investigation we would just as soon not have known. We needed to inform the synagogue leadership of this new information before they read it in the local paper.

We decided to stop using that particular scroll. Yes, we did have other scrolls to use, but somehow, the concept of "Torah" had been sullied in the process.

Word of the tainted Torah spread through the congregation and even made it to one newspaper article. It felt like our healing process had taken three giant steps backward. The core symbol of Judaism had been thrown into a dubious light. We needed to recapture the sacredness of our Torah.

In the spring of 1998, I brought to the congregation leadership the idea of commissioning a new Torah. Many congregations had engaged in the sacred act of helping to write a Torah. Many had also turned the notion of a "Torah Project" into a huge fundraising opportunity as well. The idea was embraced as just what the congregation needed.

We hired the scribe who had shared in the discomfort that night with the police to help us. While the congregation embraced this project as a noble goal and a wonderful educational opportunity for their families, it was perhaps most meaningful to those of us who knew about the desecrated Torah. Now we had a chance to start again, knowing that *this* project could not be profaned. The kick-off of the Torah project was the High Holy Days of 1998,

5759 on the Jewish calendar. Here's the sermon I gave our people on Rosh Hashanah to launch our Torah project:

> My Palm Pilot tells me it is Rosh Hashanah. It tells me I need to finish my sermons, walk the dog, pick my son up at soccer practice, take my daughter to school and, yes, remember to put new batteries in my digital organizer—my lifeline. Where would I be without my Palm Pilot? How could my busy life be organized if I didn't have my little electronic tool to keep me in check? Some would argue that my favorite pastime at synagogue board meetings is to whip out my Palm Pilot and start up a game of hearts or chess. This is not always accurate; sometimes, however, it is. I need a new pastime.
>
> Good thing for baseball! The American pastime had a resurgence this year. For the last few years we were discouraged and disillusioned by the strike, the high salaries, the whining of the players and the cost of the games. This year, though, all of that changed. People started going to games again, watching more baseball on TV—rediscovering our national pastime.
>
> The catalysts for the resurgence of baseball were three players who chased the most elusive of records. Mark McGwire, Sammy Sosa and Ken Griffey, Jr. brought the American people back to the ballpark, back to our national pastime and back to basics. As McGwire, Sosa and Griffey chased Roger Maris' record of 61 home runs in a single season, even non-baseball people turned into fans. I've watched baseball more this year than in any season past. I even watch the Phillies!

Through the efforts of the mighty three, we have rediscovered what a great game baseball is. We watch to see if a home run will be hit. But we wind up coming back even when a lousy team is playing, for the sheer joy of the game. We needed a spark to re-ignite the flame within. Baseball, we have found again, is truly the American pastime.

What then would we consider our Jewish pastime? Is there something like baseball which is basic to our identity, yet has gone seemingly unnoticed? Where do we turn to reacquaint ourselves with that which is our long-lost pastime? We turn to that which has defined us, guided us, inspired us and motivated us for thousands of years: food. Not gefilte fish, lox and bagels but food for our souls. That source of sustenance is none other than Torah.

Torah is at the center of our lives as Jews. Torah occupies the front center section of this and every sanctuary. No ritual object is more revered through prayer and song than Torah.

When one comes to Torah to share the honor of the blessings with the community, it is known literally as "going up" to Torah. Torah exists on a higher plane. It is where we strive to be, yet it is also where we begin. As Rabbi Eric Yoffie, president of the Union of American Hebrew Congregations stated in his inaugural address, "From our earliest days, the central, burning, incandescent passion of the Jew has been study. From our earliest days, the teaching of Torah has been our first duty and greatest joy. From our earliest days, to be a self-affirming Jew is to devote yourself to Jewish literacy and lifelong learning.

Therefore, our message will be: Torah. And our program will be: educate, educate, educate."

The centerpiece of this Rosh Hashanah service, as in every morning service, is the reading of Torah. We should note as well that every reading of Torah on this New Year's Day revolves around the child. Some synagogues are reading today about God taking notice of Sarah by giving her a child. Some synagogues read in the *Haftarah* about Hannah and how God remembers her with the gift of a child. We just read of the sacrifice of Isaac. Abraham learned that our God does not want the sacrifice of human life. Abraham learned that the promise for the future lies in the hands of our children. And who was it that led this congregation in the reading of Torah this morning? It was our children.

Tomorrow we will read of God as the parent of Adam and Eve. God as parent in that story could have *not* given them free will. God could have merely charted their course for them. God chose not to do this. God teaches us the importance of teaching our children, then letting them live their lives, hopefully based on the examples we have shown them. One idea is very clear in each of these biblical passages: parents must, in the words of Crosby, Stills, Nash and Young, "Teach your children well." Everything we say, every act we live out in the drama of our lives teaches our children a lesson.

The commandment to educate our children and ourselves comes to us from the very words of Torah. These words we repeat three times a day, but do we really listen to what the words say? *You shall teach these words to your children . . .* states the *Shema*. It is the obligation of parents not only to teach, but to repeat the words, teachings and stories of Torah over and over again. We must empower our children to learn from and live their lives by the words of Torah.

As parents, we need to be examples for our children. If Torah is our foundation, our Jewish pastime, then parents need to help assemble the building blocks of that foundation. When we want our kids to learn how to throw that baseball so they can participate in our national pastime, we buy them a glove, take them outside and spend hours teaching them how to throw and hit. Yet, when it comes time to teach them our Jewish pastime—the study of Torah—we drop them off and hope they learn.

Rabbi Wayne Dossick shows this pattern to us in a moving story.

> *"Come my child, come. Let me show you. This is a baseball. See how you hold it; see how you throw it. And this is a soccer ball. See how you kick it. And this is the basketball hoop that hangs on our garage. See how you shoot the ball into the hoop. And this is the field where you can play, where you can throw and hit and run and kick."*
>
> *"Why, Daddy, why?"*
>
> *"Because my child, sports will teach you how to be strong, how to be agile, how to be quick. You'll learn individual skills and the greater good of the group. You'll learn grace, both in losing and in winning. See how much I like to root for my team. See how good I feel when I play in a tough game. You'll love it too.*

*Sports will make you a man; sports will make you a woman—just like Mommy and Daddy.*

*"Come my child, come. Let me drive you to Hebrew School."*

*"Why, Daddy, why?"*

*"So that, my child, you can learn the language and the literature and the laws of your people."*

*"Daddy, can you help me with my Hebrew homework?"*

*"I'd love to, my child, but it has been so long since I've read any Hebrew—probably since my bar mitzvah. Ask Mommy, maybe she'll be able to help you."*

*"Come, my child, come. Let me drop you off at services at the synagogue."*

*"Why, Mommy? Why?"*

*"Because, my child, Shabbat is the most important of all days. You need to learn the prayers and listen to the melodies and know the traditions of your people. All your friends from Hebrew school will be there, and your teacher, and the rabbi and the cantor. You'll like it."*

*"Will you come with me, Mommy? Will you sit in services with me, Daddy?"*

*"We would like to, my child. But we are going to play tennis. And, afterward, we are going to the supermarket and the mall. You know how hard we work all week, and Saturday is our only day to relax and play, and do all the shopping. You understand, don't you? But, don't worry. We'll be back in time to pick you up right after services."*

*"Why Mommy? Why Daddy? Why?"*

"Teach these words to your children," means not only instructing our kids, not only providing a synagogue to instruct them, but teaching them by the example we set. How do we do this? Rabbi Joshua Liebman writes this commentary:

> *Give your children unconditional love, a love that is not dependent on report cards, clean hands or popularity. Give your children a sense of your wholehearted acceptance of their human frailties as well as their abilities and virtues. Give your children your permission to grow up to make their own lives independent of you. Give them a sense of truth; make them aware of themselves as citizens of a universe in which there are many obstacles as well as fulfillments. Bestow upon your child the blessings of your faith. These are the laws of honoring your son and your daughter as children are committed to honor parents.*

The love we show our children is guided by our understanding of Torah.

What is it we truly want for our children? A beautiful passage by an unknown author reads:

> *We want life and the religious understanding of it to be a joyous thing. We want our children to appreciate the beauty and the richness of our customs and ceremonies, and to observe them not out of a sense of guilt, not out of a belief in their magical quality, but rather as an expression of their own felt needs, or as part of their own recognition that a symbol or*

> *ceremony is a way of clothing ideals with flesh. We want them to understand that the custom or ceremony is not as important as the feeling tones surrounding it. We want our children to learn how to love, to love themselves and to love each other, to love humanity—for the world needs so much love. We want them to sense their bond of union with the Jewish people and with all people. We want them to look upon religion not just as something inherited, but rather as something discovered.*

Bringing our kids back to basics, back to the Jewish pastime of Torah study can help achieve these goals. What can we do? How can we all be a part of our Jewish pastime and help bring the next generation back to Torah? This year, 5759, has been dedicated by Congregation M'kor Shalom as "The Year of Our Torah." This is the 25th anniversary of Congregation M'kor Shalom. We celebrate 25 years of teaching and transmitting Torah; 25 years of living the words of Torah and being an example to our community.

During this very special year, I propose that each of us make a concerted effort to approach Torah ourselves and involve our families in the study of Torah. For baseball, we turn to The Sports Authority, Modell's and structured Little Leagues to outfit and teach us how to play. With regard to Torah, we need to turn to our synagogue and teachers. During this year of our Torah, let us put aside 20 minutes a week to study the weekly portion. That's all it takes to read through the prescribed three or four chapters that are set aside each week. If your schedule permits, come and study during the week with members of our professional staff or during the evenings with members of our community through the adult education program. Sit down with your kids and help them with their religious school and Hebrew school homework. Subscribe to a weekly *D'var* Torah on the Internet and have it sent via e-mail. Bring the beauty of your Jewish heritage into the forefront of your lives and the lives of your families.

In this year of our Torah, we will undertake a project unlike anything we have done before. We have commissioned a brand new Torah for our congregation to serve as a symbol of everything we stand for. As we speak, a scribe in the coastal city of Netanya, outside Tel Aviv, is writing our new sacred scroll. In May of this year we will dedicate this scroll in a ceremony of betrothal, under a *chuppah*, as we welcome this Torah into our midst and pledge to be better caretakers of our Jewish heritage. This Torah project provides us with an opportunity to teach our children by example and to involve our families and excite our children with Torah.

Every member of this congregation has an opportunity that comes along once in a lifetime. Every member of this congregation has a chance to fulfill one of the greatest commandments: personally helping to write a Torah. Reflect on the first time you were called to Torah. Perhaps it was your bar/bat mitzvah; perhaps it was the bar/bat mitzvah of your child or grandchild. Remember the feeling of pride. Remember the connection to the Jewish people. There are very few moments in our life that compare to those moments—those moments that surround Torah.

One of the most rewarding experiences for a rabbi is to share life-cycle ceremonies with families. As we stand next to the bar/bat mitzvah and family, or the bride and groom at their *auf rauf* or the adult learner who is reading Torah for the first time, we see people bind their lives to Torah. This year, we will bind our congregation to a new, sacred scroll.

We have designed the celebration of the Torah to enable every member of this congregation to participate. Every child can purchase a letter of Torah, forever linking them to our people, our heritage and our teachings. What a wonderful thought for the bar/bat mitzvah or the confirmand to take a small portion of their gifts and turn it into a piece of sacred text, which will forever link them to Torah. Throughout the year we will schedule opportunities to meet our local scribe, learn the art of writing a Torah, and witness him writing pieces of what will become our sacred possession.

It is my hope that everyone will participate in this most holy of projects. If your child is becoming bar/bat mitzvah this year, perhaps that moment, that moment which surrounds Torah, can be immortalized through the purchase of a verse, chapter or bar/bat mitzvah portion to be inscribed in our new Torah scroll. For what may amount to a very small percentage of the cost of the celebration, a piece of Torah—something that lasts beyond the moment, something that will teach future generations—can be forever linked to your family.

As we leave this synagogue today, ready to take a walk along the base-path of our life—ready to turn from what we were toward what we wish to be—let us ensure our inscription in the Torah, the true book of life for the Jewish people. We can lead by example. We can teach our children through our actions and commitment to our people and our synagogue.

On September 8, many of us watched Mark McGwire step up to the plate and make history with his 62nd home run of the year. Kids and parents were awed not only by his accomplishment, but by feeling they were part of something important, something rare. Everyone in this room can now step up to the plate. We may not launch a baseball 500 feet, but we can be a true hero to our kids. We can show them, by our example, that which truly defines history: the words of the Torah. Help make history! Be a part of this joyous celebration of 25 years of M'kor Shalom. As you and I expose a new generation to our pastime, our Jewish pastime, I hope we will write a new chapter in the life of our people. May this be God's will.

It had been over a two-year journey from start to finish, but the Torah project was successful. It culminated in a beautiful service of dedication in May, 1999. The Torah was held under a *chuppah,* a new wedding canopy made for this service. The wedding canopy and the cover for the Torah both reflected the image of the stained glass windows. The Torah, our renewal of the sacred, bore the memory of Carol shining brightly on its cover.

In 1995, the timing of the information that had been released by the office of the prosecutor about adultery and suspicion made it impossible not to deal with those issues during our High Holy Days, the most sacred of times. My hand had been forced. But I vowed never again to dedicate a sermon on the holiest of days to this topic.

I stayed true to that promise, but it wasn't easy. The High Holy Days of 1996 came and went without incident. There was no need to address the topic of the murder—or the rabbi for that matter—in the sermons. It was our first High Holy Days with the new assistant rabbi, and we dedicated those Holy Days to reaching inward to the people of our own congregation. We were not so lucky in '97.

September 5, 1997 is etched in my mind forever. Friday morning. Our house the usual zoo, trying to get the kids off to school. The phone rang early. An elderly congregant with whom I was very close was dying. He was a regular at my weekly Torah study class. His wife called and asked that I come to the hospital to begin the prayers for the dying at his bedside. These calls are not unusual for a rabbi, but they're never easy. I got dressed and rushed to the ICU, without an inkling that as I left my home, surprise visitors were heading toward it.

While I was at the hospital two very large men and a woman from the prosecutor's office appeared at my door. Their guns were in plain view, making them an intimidating apparition—particularly to a child. And it was my 5-year-old son who answered the door.

Apparently the agreement I had made with each of the three prosecutors working on this case was forgotten. I had said I would cooperate with them; in turn, the prosecutors had promised not to surprise me. Well, Debbi and the kids were quite surprised when she was handed two subpoenas—one for her and the other for me—to appear before the Grand Jury and testify on September 15th. Debbi explained that I was at the bedside of a dying patient and could not be reached. The officers then stated they would go to the hospital and hand me my subpoena in front of this poor family in the midst of their own crisis. Somehow she convinced them to leave my subpoena with her. She reached me by cell phone to share the news.

We were not alone. The cantor, synagogue president, and an assorted cast of characters including the rabbi's children had received subpoenas that morning. My testimony was to take place only two weeks prior to Rosh Hashanah. Once again we were to be distracted by the ugliness of the investigation. My holidays were ruined before they began.

In perhaps one of my less professional moments, I called the prosecutor's office and demanded to speak directly with him. This prosecutor was no different from those who preceded him, in that his political ambitions and the very public nature of this case seemed to drive him. But there was one thing that was significantly different. He was Jewish.

I was not looking for favoritism. I was looking for understanding and a little human decency. I explained that the congregation had come so far in the healing process, and every news story and report on TV sent people backward in that process. I was going to be paraded before a Grand Jury seeking to indict the rabbi for murder two weeks before the Holy Days. Why did this have to take place now? He stated that information had come forward which necessitated his scheduling the Grand Jury for this particular time. I did not believe him.

As it turns out, there was no compelling reason to schedule the proceedings at that time. I speculate that this prosecutor, like the others before him, knew that in September and October attention is drawn to the Jewish community because of the Jewish Holidays. Perhaps he reasoned that if he could capitalize on that already-present attention, his notoriety would increase. I had the strong impression that he felt he needed to demonstrate to the non-Jewish community that he was not biased in favor of the rabbi in any way. Trespassing on the Jewish holidays would be one way of making this sale in the arena of public opinion.

September 15th came and I was a wreck. Our synagogue attorney accompanied Debbi and me to the Grand Jury room in Camden, New Jersey. As soon as we walked off the elevator a commotion of TV cameras and reporters met us. I felt like a criminal as we were hurried down a hallway to avoid the media. We knocked on the door and were admitted to the Grand Jury room. The attorney managed to get Debbi and others from the synagogue community excused from testifying. The cantor and I, however, were not so lucky.

Grand Jury testimony is particularly stressful because it is completely controlled by the prosecutor. I was called into the jury room. I was scared, but also angry that I had to be there at a sacred time. I had decided to take a stand on principle and demand that my swearing-in take place over a Hebrew Bible, not the one I thought they would use. I had my arguments mentally lined up. I was ready for war.

"Do you swear to tell the truth?" I was asked—with no Bible at all. "Yes," I quietly answered, and sat down. So much for my stand on principle.

I did my best to answer the questions. Most of them were just as I expected. What I did not expect was that the pain would be still be so great as I recalled the night of the murder, now almost three years past.

Under Grand Jury procedure, questions can come from the prosecutor, the assistant prosecutor, or any Grand Juror. Witnesses cannot bring attorneys. The process is completely one-sided. One attorney told me that if the prosecutor wants the jury to indict a piece of bread, they will. I could not tell whether the prosecutor was looking for an indictment or if this was simply an investigative Grand Jury.

The assistant prosecutor rose to question me. He was a tall man with a long, drawn face. He looked stern, yet compassionate. He started with fairly simple questions: name, address, how many years I had worked at the synagogue, and other basics. I began to get very nervous. When I get nervous, I resort to humor. We all have our nervous habits and stress-relieving behaviors. Mine is humor. He asked me what the difference was between an assistant rabbi and an associate rabbi. In my case, the difference was that after about three years I received a paper promotion, a salary increase, and more formal responsibility within the congregation. But I answered him, "The rabbinic joke is that both titles begin with the same three letters."

There was tremendous laughter from the Grand Jury—even the prosecutor laughed. Some of the tension eased.

He asked whether it was normal for women to be attracted to and even proposition their rabbis. I explained that we see people in their most vulnerable times. It's our job to help them make it through their darkest moments in the valley of shadows. Some may confuse compassion with other emotions. Again, I resorted to humor. I said I had begun to get a complex, asking my wife, "What's wrong with me? I've been a rabbi for five years now and not a single proposition!" Another laugh filled the room.

Most of the questions were simply statements of fact: I had seen things, heard things and knew things that might be relevant to the case. I also found myself educating the Grand Jury in Jewish religion and customs.

There were things I had forgotten since the first questioning by the authorities. At one point, the assistant prosecutor asked a question and I had no recollection of the answer. He then read to the jury a statement I had given the police two and a half years before that answered the question. I had the enormously uncomfortable feeling that I appeared to be a liar. He must have seen the look on my face. Very compassionately, he assured me that many people forget details after such a long period.

The questioning took over three hours. I was emotionally and physically exhausted when I was finally excused. I knew the stress was only starting, however: outside the closed door, media throngs waited to pounce.

The door opened. Cameras rolled. The reporters could see from my face how painful this was. To my relief, most of them were respectful and professional. All except one. I looked up and once again saw the reporter from the Philadelphia Jewish paper. She seemed to be missing what all the others saw: how hard I was struggling. "Gary," she said, "Can't you answer just one question for me?" The tone of her voice, her demeanor, implied to me that I owed her something special, something the other media representatives shouldn't get, perhaps because she represented the Jewish press. I was appalled. Once again, the Jewish paper of Philadelphia struck me as blatantly disregarding Jewish values and ethics. How I wished they had taken their cue from the South Jersey Jewish paper. That publication had traveled the ethical high road, avoiding sensationalizing the story, and showing sensitivity to the synagogue by not publishing gossip or innuendo.

I went home and prepared to watch myself at 5:00, 6:00 and 11:00 on the major networks. There I was walking down the hallway. The commentators speculated about what I knew and why I was part of the investigation. I suddenly flashed on the fact that my entire congregation and community were watching these telecasts. I would have to face the crowd of 2,000 souls once again on Rosh Hashanah, all of whom would know about my grand jury appearance.

Next morning I steeled myself, then opened the papers and read the headlines. The most comical was in the *Philadelphia Daily News*. "Monday the Rabbi Talked," said the huge print. The inside page continued; ". . . but we are not privy to what Rabbi Gary Mazo shared with the Grand Jury . . ." Not a proud way to make headlines. I assured my mom that someday I would be the centerpiece of an article or two she could cut out and show her friends. These weren't the ones . . .

Nothing ever came of that Grand Jury experience. There was no indictment, no arrest, and no need to have intruded on our Holy Days. In fact, it would be almost another year until there was any resolution or even the beginning of closure.

At this point all I wanted to do was climb under a rock or run far, far away. I couldn't do either. But I could, and did, make the decision that that year's High Holy Day services would not be marred by any more talk of murder, adultery or scandal from the pulpit. I would not let the investigation rob us of what we had worked so hard to achieve.

So, we took a few steps back but prepared to take many more steps forward. The sacred had been profaned time and time again. My job was to stay focused on the sacred, and help bring it back into the life of my congregation.

CHAPTER 8

# A Bottle of Scotch

The prosecutor outdid himself during the month of preparation for the 1998 Holy Days. My last conversation with him had not been a good one. I had asked again for assurance that there would be no surprise jolts in store for the congregation during our sacred period. He declined to make such a promise. But he did say he would make every effort to give me some advance warning before "something big" happened.

September 10, 1998, started like any other Thursday. I brought my daughter with me to her pre-school class in the morning and began to prepare for my weekly Torah study class. It was only a week and a half before Rosh Hashanah and we were studying the themes of the Holy Days: repentance, prayer, charity. The ring of the phone broke my concentration. It was my secretary, with urgency in her voice. "ABC News is on the line," she said. "They want to know if you have a comment on the rabbi's arrest." Repentance, prayer, charity and hopes for a normal Thursday had been pre-empted.

We quickly brought a TV into my office and tried desperately to get reception on one of the local stations. As the picture came into focus, I picked up the phone and called the office of the prosecutor. He took my call immediately, perhaps realizing there was one phone call he had forgotten to make. Sure enough, it was another surprise blow for the people of M'kor Shalom.

Four years of frustration came out in that phone call. My voice reached decibels I didn't know I had. It was probably only through Divine intervention that the phone lines didn't melt.

Just when I thought I couldn't get any angrier, footage of the actual arrest blasted onto the TV screen. Somehow, a news crew just happened to be stationed outside the rabbi's home and had followed him as he drove away. A few blocks away from his house, police cars surrounded the rabbi's car. He was pulled out, handcuffed and shoved in the back of the police cruiser. No doubt the news show's producers were congratulating themselves on having offered great television that morning. I laid it on the line, accusing the prosecutor of tipping off the media to capture this horrendous scene, yet not having the common decency to call me at the synagogue and warn me of what was about to transpire.

I reminded the prosecutor of where we were—once again—on the Jewish calendar. He tried to assure me that the timing was purely coincidental. New information had made the arrest imperative at that moment, he asserted. I had heard that line at this season last year. Panic and crisis were now rampant in the synagogue.

Streams of people poured down the hallway to my office. Word of the arrest was on the local radio station and in the supermarkets. We had been down this road before, but never so far. Once again, I could not even begin to fathom the significance of what was happening.

A nightmare scenario, the worst possible turn this tragedy could take, was being played out before our eyes. The parking lot started filling up with news media vans from New York, Washington, and points in between. (How *do* they circle so fast?) I slipped, once again, into overdrive.

First, the practicalities of the situation had to be addressed. A substantial percentage of the Eastern seaboard-based news media was in our parking lot, and they weren't going to leave until we made some sort of statement. Knowing that whatever we said would get huge publicity, we needed to be careful. There were still supporters of the rabbi within the congregation and we didn't want them to be hurt. Also, I had continued to preach that we believe in justice, that everyone deserves an opportunity to be judged by his or her peers in court, not prejudged by the public. We couldn't contribute to a rush to judgment.

There were also the rabbi's children to think of. They had lost their mother; now their father was being accused of the murder. What must they be feeling? Their needs had to be considered. On the other hand, I had maintained a very close relationship with Carol's family. They desperately needed closure. While the arrest was by no means the end of the story, perhaps it was the beginning of the road to closure for them.

All these issues as well as our own personal sense of disbelief and crisis were taken into consideration as we pondered what to say. Once again, my office was a war room. We plotted strategy while overwhelmed with emotion. We tried to focus on the community, but each of us was torn by our individual hurt. The synagogue president, the head of the local Jewish Federation, a public relations specialist and her husband (who was also a past president of the congregation) joined us. We tried to write the correct words to say publicly.

On television, the prosecutor had appeared for a news conference. Footage of the arrest was shown again. The prosecutor stood in the spotlight stating that in his opinion the rabbi was responsible for Carol's death. The charges were murder and conspiracy to commit murder.

Then a haunting image flashed on the screen: the rabbi in an orange prison jumpsuit with his hands shackled behind his back. Whether he was a criminal or not, he looked the part at that moment. The prosecutor told the cameras he had just gotten off the phone and assured someone (me) that the timing and proximity of the arrest to the Jewish holidays was purely accidental. Events had forced him to make the arrest at this time. He announced that the rabbi was being held on $400,000 bail.

To see the rabbi in prison garb was a tormenting and incomprehensible vision. How could someone who had so much, who was on top of his professional world, who was surrounded by a loving family, *who had been a trusted and revered spiritual leader,* be reduced to what we were seeing? Many of us in the room were in tears. For so long we had been trying not to harbor preconceived notions of guilt or innocence. We may have been badly disillusioned by the revelations about his personal life, but murder was something else entirely. Yet there he was, facing charges that could lead to spending the rest of his life in prison.

Or worse. What if the prosecutor asked for the death penalty? How would those who knew and loved the rabbi deal with that? Even if he was guilty, the thought of a potential execution was terrifying.

The memories that orange jumpsuit conjured up! Four years earlier, on the Jewish holiday of Purim, we saw the rabbi in a familiar outfit. At Purim, Jews read the book of

Esther and celebrate our escape from execution and expulsion in Persia. The wicked Haman had a plan to destroy us, but the heroes Mordecai and Queen Esther saved us from destruction. We turn everything on its head on Purim and wildly celebrate freedom and life. We also dress up in costumes. The rabbi had a yearly outfit that included the shedding of various layers of silly clothes, causing much laughter. The outer garment was an old, orange jumpsuit. Many of us had pictures of him wearing that orange jumpsuit with our kids on his lap. Now none of us were laughing.

The emotions of those few hours were as intense as any during this long ordeal. Some of us had feared that arrest. Many expected it. None of us had ever known an accused murderer before. Most of us were guilty of prejudging those we saw on TV in similar situations. We would look disgustingly on the accused in the orange jumpsuit and mutter something distasteful under our breath. Now the person in the jumpsuit on TV was the former spiritual leader of thousands of us. The wounds of the past four years were ripped open by the arrest.

We drafted a statement we believed was fair, honest and caring. We elected our public relations specialist, a sincere, sensitive woman, to be our spokesperson. She had the advantage of knowing most of the media people, and we hoped they would deal with her kindly.

She spoke beautifully. She spoke about hoping and praying for closure for the families involved. She spoke about not prejudging, and believing in justice. She gave no indication of whether she or any of us felt the rabbi was guilty. She simply said we hope and pray for justice. Then she took some questions, and soon the press began to go away.

In the midst of the chaos the synagogue office administrators had called down and asked what they could do. I told them there was really nothing they could do, but I could sure use a drink. I was just trying to get some emotional relief through a little facetious humor. But when I returned from watching the press conference later that morning, there was a brown bag on my desk. I opened it and found a small bottle of Chivas Regal. I appreciated their gesture.

That bottle of Scotch sits on the shelf of my office to this very day. It is a reminder of that horrible day and of the pain of the arrest of my former mentor—and of the wonderful people who helped me get through it. When people ask about it, as they often do, I share with them that it will be opened only when there is closure to this terrible chapter.

So there it sits, unopened. And I wait. A simple bottle of Scotch—a symbol of pain and hope.

Thursday afternoon: where had the day gone? Many people had come to the synagogue expressing disbelief and pain. Yet their pain seemed a bit softened by time. Perhaps they had already convicted the rabbi in their hearts and this was merely an affirmation of their own conclusions. For others, the pain was palpable and unrelieved. They would not, could not believe this was happening.

Another Friday night was coming. I needed to wrestle again with how to meet the needs of a bruised community.

This was a very different congregation from the one I had faced after Carol's murder four years before. Members had left, new ones had joined. The majority of the current membership had never had a significant relationship with Fred Neulander. I was the rabbi they knew and trusted. But many of those who did know the rabbi and were still affected by what happened in his life would be at Friday night services. I had made a promise to the congregation and to myself that I would never again devote a full sermon to our tragic topic. But the rabbi's arrest would be troubling everyone's mind; something had to be said.

I decided to address the issue head-on at the beginning of our worship service. My words, which were purely extemporaneous and heartfelt, were excerpted in a story in next morning's *Philadelphia Inquirer.* The paper reported:

> *Last night, as congregants at M'kor Shalom wrestled with the news of the rabbi's arrest Thursday on charges of conspiring to murder his wife, Rabbi Mazo sought to ease the shock. "Yesterday, the news of the day brought back one of the most painful moments in my life, and that was the death of Carol Neulander," Rabbi Mazo said. "It brought back pain and anguish and grief."*
>
> *And as he did three years ago, Rabbi Mazo said M'kor Shalom would be a sanctuary from that pain, and true to its name, which in Hebrew means "source of peace." It would be a place where the community could rise above the innuendo and gossip. This time, however, Rabbi Neulander was not at services.*
>
> *Free on $400,000 bail after pleading not guilty, he spent the day confined to his home yesterday. Most family members and friends stayed away. Neighbors gathered on the street in front of his house but dared not approach. Even his attorneys did not think it necessary to visit.*

> *"He is subdued and bewildered, still certainly very unable to believe this is happening," said one of his attorneys. "He never thought this day would come, that they would bring charges against him."*
>
> *At the synagogue, there was little talk of the congregation's former leader, and in his brief remarks, Rabbi Mazo cautioned against a rush to judgment. "This synagogue will continue to be what it always has been," the rabbi said: "A place of peace. And a place of strength."*

I made the decision, perhaps selfishly, not to deliver a formal sermon that night. I also remembered the power of the cantor's music through our most difficult moments. I asked that she use the slot held for the sermon to play some of that healing music. Without putting into words the pain and continued need for healing, the music allowed us to think of just those things. It was a difficult night, yet not as difficult as the Friday after the resignation and clearly not as difficult as the Friday after Carol's death. The synagogue was in a different place now. I knew they would be OK. This was heart-wrenching for many, yet it was no longer about the synagogue as an institution. The dreadful pall I had first sensed in March of 1995 had slowly—excruciatingly slowly—thinned and drifted away.

CHAPTER 9

# Endings and Beginnings

By January of 1998, the congregation had achieved a renewed sense of normalcy. We were planning and executing new and vibrant programming. People were worshipping on Friday evenings in larger numbers than ever before. There was wonderful chemistry among the professional staff; we were friends as well as colleagues. I was settling into my role leading one of South Jersey's largest congregations.

I had just turned 34 years old and had reached what many in my field defined as the ultimate professional success. I was senior rabbi at a synagogue that fell into the largest size category of Reform Judaism congregations. Most rabbis who aspire to such positions don't achieve them until their early 50s.

The quandary for me was that this was not how I had defined success. There were many problems with a large congregation. Certainly, there were also benefits that could only be had with a larger community. Yet something was missing in my life and I was only now, after three and a half years in the job, beginning to put my finger on it.

The most troubling issue was that the congregation and the demands it placed on me had swallowed up my life. I was no longer a reliable partner to my wife or a readily available dad to my kids. I had always prided myself on my involvement as a father. Now my kids were starting to resent my job, and that made my heart ache. I was missing the kids' soccer games with regularity, and sharing their evening homework sessions was a thing of the past. I was out at meetings or teaching classes or officiating at services five to seven nights a week. The usual "date night" Debbi and I had scheduled to preserve sanity and romance in our marriage had long gone by the wayside.

I had seen these problems developing two years before, and had realized that they were dangerous. But I hadn't fixed the problems or done anything constructive to mitigate them. With all the frantic events and requirements that had enveloped us, it wasn't until this point that we were able to take a step back, analyze the path we were traveling—and realize the void.

When we were whirling in chaos and crisis, we adjusted and moved in the necessary directions. We never had time to examine the implications of my actions on our family. And when we finally took that inward look, we found tough and troubling issues that demanded immediate attention.

My wife was angry. She was angry about the virtual disappearance of her husband and partner from family domestic life. And she had never had the opportunity to express that anger, feeling that she would be putting additional pressure on my already pressure-packed life. So it stayed inside, boiling unhealthily in her with no outlet.

Perhaps most difficult for me was the time I had missed with my daughter. Sara had been born in the midst of the tumult in April of 1995, and the first two years of her life are a blur. I didn't know her the way I needed to—and the way she needed me to. She was my little princess and she loved me dearly, but I knew I was letting her down.

After a particularly difficult weekend where Debbi and I were treated as unwelcome guests in our own congregation, something prophetic occurred. Debbi opened up our monthly rabbinic newsletter and saw that my ultimate dream position in Cape Cod was available. She cried out and ran into the kitchen. "This is it!" she exclaimed. She reminded me of my professional goals and we talked about making a change. That day was a catalyst for some real soul-searching.

The pain of the last three and a half years had been slowly coming to the surface. Now it came out in full force. Our lives had been utterly disrupted by the prolonged crisis. Our plans had been put on indefinite hold. Our kids had suffered, our marriage had suffered and our individual professional goals had suffered. We were tired. I was doing what many rabbis said they wanted to do. But my soul-searching made me confront the truth: inside, I was miserable.

My anger at Fred Neulander began to come out as well. I had arrived there to work with him, learn from him—then leave and realize my own goals. Yes, I know life doesn't always conform to our expectations, and no one could have foreseen the gruesome twists in the path ahead. But it was through the rabbi's conduct that I had inherited a grieving community in pain, and been given the awesome task of trying to heal the wounds he had inflicted.

On the other hand (as all good rabbis would say), things had worked out well in several respects. I had been able to respond to the challenge, receive the trust of our synagogue members, and effect real change in a large congregation. They had given me a wonderful opportunity, and I was proud of what we had accomplished together. Yet I still needed to leave, and this would be difficult.

I decided to call the central New York office and officially apply for the Cape Cod position. I was up many nights wrestling with this decision. I sought counsel from my rabbinic advisers, most of whom had told me to get out three years before. Without exception, they counseled me to actively pursue this opportunity, to reach for my own definition of success. The thought filled me with tremendous guilt. I worried that I might be abandoning a community in need. The reality was, however, that they were fine and would be fine with or without me. My ego had to accept that fact.

I applied for and was ultimately offered my dream job. We decided to put our family first and take this wonderful opportunity as a sign from God that it was time to make big changes. The difficult part was telling the congregation. I shared the news first with a dear friend who at that time was president of the congregation. He had known I was applying for the position, and had rightly assumed that if it were offered I would take it.

After tears from both of us, we planned the best way to notify our congregation that there would be yet another change in their leadership. One positive aspect was that I would not start my new position until July of 1999, 15 months away. Even though the Cape Cod community was in need of immediate rabbinic services, I made the job acceptance conditional on a full year of transition at M'kor Shalom. I had worked too hard and too long to ensure their success as a congregation. I wasn't about to change that now, and I wanted to be certain they would have adequate time to find my successor.

We decided I would compose a letter to the entire congregation, and we would call a special meeting of the board of trustees so I could give them the news. Before the meeting, I had an uncontrollable urge to call Rabbi Neulander and let him hear directly from me what was happening. Why did I need to call him? I guess I still cared about him. I needed him to know I was remaining true to my original goals. I told him I was leaving and his words to me were: "Don't tell me you found your 300 families in Cape Cod?" He wished me luck.

At the meeting, I read the letter which would arrive in the mailboxes of our congregants the next day to the board of trustees:

> The Torah is filled with dreams and dreamers. Often it is the realization of a dream that redefines the life of a Patriarch or Matriarch. We know that Jacob dreamed of a ladder with its top reaching the heavens. His dream helped him reach new spiritual heights and facilitated personal growth. Jacob, again, wrestled with the angel until dawn. After his struggles he emerged a new person: confident, wiser, more humble and able to move forward and fulfill his calling in life.
>
> Over the last eight years at M'kor Shalom I have counseled many of you in reference to your own dreams, goals and ambitions. I believe in constantly evaluating

one's life and looking deep inside to see if one's values and practices are in sync with each other. Now, after three rewarding and educational years as the senior rabbi of Congregation M'kor Shalom I have thought of my own rabbinic and familial dreams.

These past few years have taught me many lessons. At times, I felt very much alone in the midst of our challenges. I learned quickly that I was not alone. In front of me stood a special congregation willing to work with me to bring healing to our community. I learned of the unique bond and partnership between congregation and rabbi. We all grew and learned from this experience. Now I feel I can move forward and pursue my dreams. I have always felt that my personality, my skills and my heart are best suited to serve a smaller community. I have often hoped for such an opportunity in the New England area.

I have been selected, and am now in final negotiations, for the position of rabbi of The Cape Cod Synagogue in Hyannis, Massachusetts. I will begin July 1, 1999. This has been a difficult decision for my family and me. Debbi and I know, however, that it is the right decision for our family. We are delaying moving on until July of 1999 so that I can help facilitate a smooth transition to the next senior rabbi of this congregation.

With the wise guidance of our leadership and the help of the UAHC, I am confident that the right individual will be found for this very special congregation. We all learned three years ago that no one rabbi defines a congregation. A congregation gains its character and strength from its membership. This congregation is truly blessed with a strong, diverse and committed membership base.

> I thank you for the past eight years. I thank you for the trust and love you have shown my family and me. Cherry Hill will always be home for us and we will cherish moments spent here. I look forward to moving ahead, very proud of what I have accomplished here, and anticipating forming new bonds of partnership and friendship. *B'shalom.*

It was a difficult meeting and a difficult letter to write. But it was profoundly cleansing to know I was moving on, even if not for a full year. The decision had been made.

That last year on the job was difficult. Change and transition, even for positive reasons, are not easy. It was in the midst of that transitional year that the rabbi was arrested and charged with the murder of his wife. At that moment, my gut told me I would have to change my plans and once again help this congregation through crisis. But this crisis was not as profound as the storm three years earlier. The story was no longer about the congregation. They would be fine.

I thought long and hard about what to say in the last Yom Kippur sermon I would ever give this congregation. I had made the definite decision that the arrest or the murder would not be the main focus. I had a unique opportunity to say goodbye to a community I had grown close to and truly loved. I had one last chance, on our most solemn Holy Day, to touch individuals with whom I had shared many key moments. I wanted to communicate my decision to pursue a more balanced life in a way that might help others going through the same struggle. I decided to write my Yom Kippur sermon in the loose form of an ethical will to my congregation: a goodbye with an invitation for each of them to search their own souls, to reach for balance in their own lives:

> We were at our summer haven, one of our favorite and one of the most peaceful places on earth: Camp Harlam. Many of you know that Debbi and I have been spending summers at Camp Harlam since before we were ordained as rabbis. This summer was difficult for us, because it was our final two weeks at this special place. It was the last night of camp and we were gathered in the dining hall for the final banquet. The theme of the banquet was the 40th anniversary of Camp Harlam. The night was festive and celebratory. As the evening came to a close, the song leader led the camp in the "top 10" countdown of the summer's favorite songs. She came to song number four. I listened to the words of Harry Chapin's "Cat's in the Cradle." At that moment, I happened to be at my son Ari's table, sitting with my eight-year-old on my knee. We listened and sang along with the music.
>
> *A child arrived just the other day,*
> *Came to the world in the usual way,*
> *But there were planes to catch*
> *And bills to pay,*
> *He learned to walk while I was away*
> *He was talking before I knew it and as he grew*
> *he said I'm going to be like you Dad,*
> *you know I'm going to be like you.*

*Chorus :*
*And the cat's in the cradle,*
*And the silver spoon, Little Boy Blue,*
*And the Man in the Moon,*
*When you coming home dad, I don't know when*
*We'll get together then, you know we'll have a good time then.*

*My son turned 10 just the other day,*
*Said thanks for the ball now c'mon let's play*
*Will you teach me to throw, I said not today,*
*I've got a lot to do, he said that's OK*
*And he walked away and he smiled and he said*
*You know I'm going to be like you, Dad,*
*you know I'm going to be like you.*

As we got to the next verse, Ari turned to me, sadness in his eyes, and said,"That sounds just like you, Dad." After I pulled the knife out of my heart, he added: "But you decided to change things so that won't continue to be you." At that moment my heart knew even more strongly that we had made the right decision.

These High Holy Days, your rabbis have been emphasizing that the world is sustained by three things: Torah, loving deeds and *avodah*. The word *avodah* is sometimes translated as worship; it is also translated as service. We each *serve* many different constituencies: our employers, our employees, our families and our God. At times it is difficult to know whom to serve first. What should our priority be? Service to our employer? Service to our families? Service to God? Service to ourselves? Can these separate services be inclusive of each other? Yes, but only when the priorities of our service are in sync with our own values. My brief encounter with Ari during that Harry Chapin song reinforced this important lesson for me. It is, and must be, our values which guide and determine the kinds of service we choose and the way we demonstrate those commitments.

It's hard to believe, but these are my ninth High Holy Days at M'kor Shalom, and they have brought me a strong feeling of bittersweet nostalgia. M'kor Shalom has been home. Debbi and I have been blessed to be in this community with family and dear friends. Yet our life is in need of change. My kids are growing up quickly, but not as much "before my eyes" as I had envisioned. I miss them. Debbi has made many sacrifices over the last few years, not the least of which was giving up her career because of the demands of mine. While she spends her time at home, I do not see her as much as I need to. And I have had precious little time for myself over these last four years—time for my own physical and mental health and well-being.

So, I must make a change. It is for these reasons, for all I miss and need to regain, that I have accepted a new position at a smaller congregation in Hyannis, Massachusetts.

As I share my last High Holy Day sermon with my M'kor Shalom family, I think of all we have accomplished and shared with one another, what I have learned, and what my dream is for Congregation M'kor Shalom. This is, essentially, my ethical will for Congregation M'kor Shalom. I have learned many lessons during my years here. I have had some wonderful successes and some difficult failures. I feel as though I have made a difference here and I know that I have grown as a rabbi—as *your* rabbi.

What have we accomplished and shared with one another? I began my service to M'kor Shalom eight years ago when this was a congregation of 600 families. We had outgrown our previous facility and were in need of new space so we could pursue the programmatic and educational goals of the congregation. Before I settled into my office at Church and Fellowship, I was packing my boxes again and moving them to 850 Evesham Road.

True to form, we expanded quickly to fill up our new home. Our school, due to its reputation for excellence and its leadership, became the largest in the Delaware Valley. We offer educational opportunities that other synagogues just can't equal. Children at M'kor Shalom do not become Hebrew school dropouts after seventh grade. They continue their education through twelfth grade, and many select college courses in Jewish studies. We added the Israel trip component to the confirmation year and something magical happened: kids became even more connected to their Jewish identity.

When we moved into this building, we inherited the region's most highly acclaimed pre-school. As the father of three who have gone through the program, I assure you that not enough accolades can be given to express the greatness of the M'kor Shalom pre-school. Directed by one of our own, this program instills—at the youngest of ages—a love for Judaism, a strong Jewish identity and a connection to Jewish life.

As we grow, we all work together to hold fast to the qualities that make this synagogue a family of families. We make a real effort to keep intimacy and warmth in spite of our nearly 4,000 members. One way we have succeeded is by creating possibly more committees and sub-committees than any synagogue I have ever known! Are you a young adult? A senior? An empty-nester? A member of an interfaith couple, or a Jew by choice? Whatever your primary definition of yourself and your needs in the synagogue, an auxiliary or committee awaits you.

We have gained national recognition for our social action programming. We have taught our community, our region and the country that social action is not just a nice thing to participate in; it is part of the *mandate* of being Jewish. Reform Judaism is predicated on the prophetic ideals of justice, mercy, kindness and sharing. We live those values through the work we have done and will continue to do in our community.

Despite our size, I believe that another of our successes is the accessibility of our clergy. Yes, we are the only clergy in town with beepers, car phones, voice mail and e-mail; the lines of communication are always open. We do our best to respond as quickly as possible and to be there for you in times of need as well as times of joy. During one of Rabbi Elder's first weeks here, he was a little taken aback when we were on one of our all-too-rare golf outings and the beeper went off just as I was trying to chip for a birdie—which many of you know does not happen that often. It was, of course, the funeral home. I handed Rabbi Elder the phone and he told the funeral director to give him the info while I chipped. I missed. However, we were able to respond and be there for this family.

Another important way we have succeeded in making this large synagogue feel smaller and more responsive is through the work of *M'kor Rachamim*. In just one year, we have hosted bereavement groups for those in need; reached out to the sick with trained volunteers; trained new shiva minyan leaders and pastoral visitors; and provided a mechanism for helping families prepare for shiva arrangements. We have provided wheelchair cutouts in the sanctuary, hearing assist units, and the ability to broadcast services in the homes of those who are ill. We are becoming one of only a handful of congregations that is certified as truly accessible to everyone.

We have revisited our bylaws twice since I have been here. The first time we took great strides in welcoming non-Jewish partners of intermarriages. We adapted ritual policy, membership policy, and took down some of the perceived iron bars that were hanging on our doors. The second time, we redefined the family and took steps to make M'kor Shalom a congregation that welcomes all Jews as family units, regardless of sexual orientation. This year I officiated at my first commitment ceremony outside the walls of M'kor Shalom. It is my hope that in the near future such ceremonies will grace this *bima* as well.

During my years here I have learned much about myself. I know that I can be and have been a good rabbi. I have also struggled with and learned how to balance my time between professional and personal demands. I have learned from my partners on this talented staff. Each has shared his or her skills and knowledge, helping me become a more complete rabbi. I have learned that the synagogue can be not only a house of prayer, but also a house of study and a house of communal gathering.

From you, I have learned why I answered the call to become a rabbi. You have given me the opportunity to be with you and spiritually guide you during the most significant moments in your lives. No other profession affords that kind of opportunity. You and I have a special connection because I shared your tears beside your loved one's grave; because I have been blessed to stand under the *chuppah* with you and your children; because I have consecrated meaningful moments in the lives of your children from birth to bar/bat mitzvah to confirmation. We have shared life's most precious moments, and I have learned about myself as a rabbi and as a person through each and every one of those moments.

I have also learned what it means to walk through the dark valley. Almost four years ago, my life and your lives were changed forever when Carol Neulander was killed. Her loss touched us all very deeply. My relationship with Carol, Fred and the Neulander family went back long before my tenure at M'kor Shalom. When Carol died, I faced the most difficult moment in my rabbinic life. I needed to help ease others' grief while my own world was dark. When Rabbi Neulander resigned in February of 1995, my rabbinic foundation crumbled.

I came to this congregation to work with Fred Neulander. He was my mentor and I am a better rabbi due to his teachings. During those first months I was disillusioned, angry and confused about where to turn and what to do. I was alone, as rabbi, with a thousand families in pain. My wife was seven months pregnant with our third child and I felt my life had been turned upside down. Yet we bonded together, as a congregation and a family of families, to support one another through our communal trauma.

We survived and we thrived. We did so because we are a family. We looked into the dark shadows and found light. Yes, the events of two weeks ago saddened us once more. I feel the loss of Carol again. I feel the wounds open again. We will weather this latest storm with the strength and dignity which has carried us through these last four years.

Let us always remember, though, the beauty of the life that was Carol Neulander. We pray for closure. We pray for peace for her family and peace for us, Carol's family of families.

These last four years have taken a toll on my life as a rabbi, a husband, a father, and an individual. But I grew in ways that will make me a better rabbi, husband and father. As I take these experiences with me, I share with you now my hopes and dreams for you.

My first hope is that you extend to your new rabbis the same respect, love and friendship that have been showered upon us over the years. I know that it is difficult to start anew, to open up again. But new relationships can be exciting, energizing and rejuvenating. Your new rabbis will be the ones who will stand by your side during the precious moments to come. Extend yourselves. Trust again. Their success is in your hands.

May M'kor Shalom continue to be a "light unto the nations" through its work in issues of social justice and social action. We are part of the larger community. The work we do is God's work. May you find new ways of reaching out to meet even greater needs.

May this congregation find a solution to what I call the crisis of Shabbat. We have essentially given the Saturday part of Shabbat over completely to the bar/bat mitzvah. While this life-cycle event is key in our lives as Jews, Shabbat is more important. The bar/bat mitzvah now seems to run our synagogue. I pray that our leaders discover a way to bring our people back to the synagogue on Shabbat morning without feeling that they're intruding on someone else's service. May Shabbat once again belong to God and the *entire* community.

May M'kor Shalom continue to reach inward and make itself a true "caring community." May we be able to respond when one of our own is in need. May we continue to establish a network of support so that when tragedy strikes or needs arise, members of this congregation feel as though they are truly part of a small family that cares about them. It is my hope and prayer that members of this synagogue never have to worry about whether their home will be prepared for shiva or whether anyone will be there to wish them "Shabbat Shalom" after they return from the hospital.

May this congregation truly become one of inclusion for all who seek the presence of God and an open Jewish community. May there be no barriers to the physically disabled. May there be no barriers to the mentally disabled. May there be no barriers to any Jew or Jewish family who seeks to join our community and call M'kor Shalom home.

May this congregation be, as our prayer book states, . . . *a doorway to a richer and more meaningful life.* My life is richer for having been your rabbi these past eight years. My rabbinate has been meaningful. This year will be exciting as well as bittersweet for me. I have looked hard at the *avodah* in my life, the people and places I serve, and have made some difficult decisions. It has taken a while, but my values and personal practices are becoming more in sync.

I thank you for the opportunity to be your rabbi. I thank you for the trust and friendship you have shown me. I pray that this year affords a smooth transition into the next stage of the life of M'kor Shalom. May it be a year for us all to focus on *avodah*—serving our families, serving our God, serving ourselves and serving this very special synagogue family. May this be God's will.

As I concluded my sermon, I experienced a sudden flash of insight: that complete healing for this congregation could *only* occur with my leaving. For many I was a link to the past, tied inextricably to the rabbi as his protégé. Some had viewed me as almost a savior. Others had heaped misplaced anger upon me. To most, I was a helpful link in the chain of this congregation's history. I had served as a bridge over a turbulent river, leading to unknown but promising new territory. They would move forward and so would I. All of us would benefit from new beginnings. But I had to leave to create the open space for those new beginnings to take root.

Tears, hugs and kind words flowed. We grieved together the parting that was about to take place. Most wished me luck and thanked me for what I had done. Others were angry at what they perceived as a selfish decision to leave. That day we began the process of saying goodbye in a healthy and honest way. One journey was coming to a close; a new journey would begin.

Moving day came sooner than I had imagined. The transition had been smooth and my successor was ready to take over. As the truck was being loaded at my house there was one more goodbye I needed to say. I drove to the home of my one-time mentor, the rabbi.

As I pulled up to the driveway, visions of all I had shared with this man at this home scorched through my mind. I remembered the holiday dinners. I also remembered the night of the murder and the otherworldly experience of the murder scene. All was quiet now. The trees were in full bloom and it was a warm day. I knocked on the door. He answered. He wished me luck and we embraced. It was different from our last embrace. I wasn't sure why I needed to say goodbye; I guess it was for my own sense of closure. He was genuine in his hopes for my success, and I was genuine in my hopes that this be a better year for him and his family.

As I made my way back to the car it all seemed again as unreal as a dreamscape. I was leaving him, his family, and the congregation he had started. Hopefully, I was leaving some of the pain and anguish behind as well. I was moving on; he was standing still. I was reaching for my dreams, and he was about to begin fighting for his life. It was very sad. He truly had nothing. And although much of it was his own doing—maybe all of it was his own doing—it was still so tragic.

CHAPTER 10

# Seeking Closure

In many ways it's a Greek tragedy set in modern life. All the elements the American public seems to crave in its news are here: power, sex, murder and the fall of a hero. It is a media-juicy story, to be sure.

Somehow, it doesn't seem believable despite the grievous fact that it's true.

The rabbi was the man who had everything—or so it seemed. He was blessed with a beautiful family, a loving wife, respect and admiration. He was at the top of his career. He could bask in the pride of having taken this small, fledgling congregation from meeting in a little schoolhouse to becoming a powerhouse in the greater Philadelphia area. He took them to their own building, then to an edifice of great beauty and size on the prestigious east side of Cherry Hill.

He touched thousands of lives during his tenure. Whether it was at bar/bat mitzvah ceremonies, or baby-namings, or weddings, or even funerals, he made a difference in the lives of many. He was there at their most significant moments, and they would never forget that.

No one knows for sure what goes on inside another person's mind, but here's my best guess. The intimidation he was able to inflict on others through his intellectual and physical power eventually led to arrogance; perhaps to narcissism; perhaps to hubris. He went beyond the rules that applied to lesser people—the ego trap that has destroyed so many charismatic leaders. He felt invincible. He began to test his invincibility. Harmless flirtations turned into illicit relationships. Other women, beautiful women, communicated their interest in him and their attraction to him. He became available. He acted on the fantasies and betrayed the trust of thousands. Rumors and suspicions became validated; but only after tragedy.

An entire community grieved with the rabbi. They mourned the loss of his wife and tried to give him strength through their love and support. They suffered betrayal beyond anything imaginable in the life of a faith community. Somehow, they survived. They reached deep into their tradition and their faith, joined hands and gave each other strength.

They learned that in crisis, some abandon ship and some try their hardest to keep it from sinking. They learned that in tragedy they could find strength. They looked deep into the flames, and like Moses, they found the presence of God. The bush was burning—yet it did not consume them.

Did Carol know about the affairs? Did she threaten to divorce the rabbi after finding out about one of the relationships? Did she condone his behavior? Did she know her killer? These may be eternal mysteries. She took her answers to her grave.

But the biggest open questions are: who *did* kill Carol—and why? We need that closure. The rabbi has been charged with hiring someone to kill her. Our tradition preaches justice and innocence until guilt is proven. For many, judgment has been made and the rabbi has been convicted. For others, this is too much to believe.

The evidence that has been released to the public, and even that to which I am privy, is still somewhat circumstantial. It is possible we will never know the full truth.

Two weeks before I left New Jersey I officiated at a funeral in the cemetery where Carol is buried. After the funeral, I walked over to her grave, placed a small rock on the headstone and prayed. I prayed for closure for her family. I prayed for truth and justice. I prayed that my prayers would be answered soon.

The tragedy took a toll on my family and me. I, too, looked within that burning bush and somehow found strength, through the presence of God and the community standing with me, to move through this crisis. I faced challenges and opportunities the likes of which I hope never to face again. One of these tragedies is one too many. Eventually, the fury and the duration of the flames began to consume the bush that was my life. For the good of my family, my soul and my community I reached a point where I needed to extricate myself from the flames and find some peace.

Now I have been blessed with the opportunity to touch and be touched by a new community. My family has achieved a healthier balance. I make the soccer games, and even get to help coach the teams. I don't expect my son will have to find "Cat's in the Cradle" playing on the local classic rock station to remind me what the right priorities are and what really counts.

I will never forget the wonderful people who shared this passage through the flames. I will always be stronger, my life always richer, for having journeyed with them. May we all find the strength to move through the crises we face in our lives. May we all grow from the experiences life throws our way. May we never have to endure the pain and anguish that Carol's family and Congregation M'kor Shalom endured. May we be blessed with health, contentment with our lot, spiritual fulfillment, and peace. Amen.

# Epilogue

I finished writing this book and sent it to the publisher in March, 2000. The rabbi's trial was scheduled to start in June, and I anticipated it would probably be over before the book was published. Toward the end of the book, I had written, "The evidence that has been released to the public, and even that to which I am privy, is still somewhat circumstantial. It is possible we will never know the full truth." While I did expect some new details to surface at the trial, I didn't think there could possibly be any remaining bombshells.

How wrong I was.

On Monday, May 1, 2000, exactly five and a half years after Carol's death, two men were arrested and charged with killing her. They have both confessed to their parts in the crime. Both claim it was a murder-for-hire, and that the person who hired them was Rabbi Fred Neulander. Both have pleaded guilty and are awaiting sentencing. Apparently their sentences will depend in part on the usefulness of their testimony in Rabbi Neulander's trial.

Based on these new facts, Camden County prosecutors upgraded the charges against the rabbi to capital murder, and announced their intention to seek the death penalty. On Wednesday, June 21, 2000, his bail was revoked and he was locked in a seven-by-ten-foot jail cell to await his rescheduled trial. In August, the rabbi's attorneys requested a change of venue, claiming the rabbi could not get a fair trial in Camden County. The trial will probably happen—somewhere—in the spring of 2001.

These new revelations hit me hard. One of the confessed killers is a man I came to know well. Soon after Carol was killed, he claimed to be a private investigator hired by the rabbi to "find the truth." I spent many hours with him in my office hypothesizing about the crime during his "investigation."

And so we continue to wait. Perhaps the trial will yield final answers. But it may produce still more questions. What we do know now is that the state is seeking the death penalty against a man of the cloth, for what may be the first time in modern American history.

Rabbi Neulander has said many times that he trusts the system to bring forth justice. I pray that he is correct. Whatever the outcome, may the full truth be revealed, and may it lead to justice and the peace of closure for all who have suffered. I pray as well that all touched by this horror can still find belief in the inherent goodness of the humanity God placed on this earth.

*Gary Mazo*
*Barnstable, Massachusetts*
*October, 2000*